NANCY'S GREEN & EASY KITCHEN

NANCY'S GREEN & EASY KITCHEN

NANCY BIRTWHISTLE

ONE BOAT

WASTE NOT, WANT NOT

I cannot throw away food, I never want to waste a morsel, and then I read about the amount of food discarded by supermarkets, shops and households. Not only does this waste our own money, it increases food prices, as supermarkets up their prices to compensate for the cost to dump it. Not to mention all of that work done by farmers and factories to produce the food in the first place, and the effect on the environment as more and more is dumped into landfill sites.

I wonder why so often we buy more than is needed in the first place? I try now to resist those 'just in case anybody comes!'-type purchases and buy instead what I need rather than what I want. I realise this is easier said than done – there are now only two of us in the house. I remember when I had a house full of hungry teenagers – the fridge and cupboards never seemed to be full. Well, full of what they said they wanted to eat!

I carefully consider leftovers before deciding to throw them away or think of them as being of no use.

GOLDEN BREADCRUMBS

MAKES 1 450G (1LB) JAR

There are numerous recipes for using up leftover or stale bread, and blitzing the bread into fresh breadcrumbs then popping them into the freezer to use from frozen is a great tip. The problem with this, I have found, is that I forget they are there. Freezing is great but labelling and dating is more important, as is remembering what you have.

I used to buy ready-to-use golden breadcrumbs that were shelf-stable and much more versatile and convenient when it came to breadcrumbing home-made foods, such as Fish Fingers (page 118), Chicken Kyiv (page 134), Curried Ham Croquettes (page 24) and Fishcakes (page 19). My home-blitzed frozen breadcrumbs didn't quite hit the spot, being too wet and not quite fine enough – and lacking colour and flavour. So I decided to spend extra time to make my own shelf-stable golden breadcrumbs. Easy, cheap and always to hand.

Once thoroughly dried, a jar of golden breadcrumbs will keep for up to 6 months. No artificial colours, flavours or preservatives.

250g stale bread
¼ tsp ground turmeric
½ tsp paprika (see Tip)

You will need:
Digital weighing scales
Bread knife
Chopping board
Food processor with
    blade attached
Lipped baking tray
    or roasting tray
Sheet of reusable
    baking parchment
Storage jar

TIP
I made my own jar of delicious 'home-grown' paprika using dried and then blitzed-up red pepper skins!

Cut the bread into cubes then pop into the bowl of a food processor and blitz to a fine crumb. Add the turmeric and paprika and blitz again for a few seconds to mix.

Transfer to the lipped baking tray lined with a sheet of reusable baking parchment.

Preheat the oven to 100°C/80°C fan/210°F/gas ¼. Bake for 2–3 hours, or until the crumbs feel hard and no longer stick to the hands. It is important that the breadcrumbs are thoroughly dried and free flowing – any residual moisture and they will go mouldy in the jar.

Allow to cool on the tray then use the baking parchment as an aid to transfer back into the food processor. Blitz again for a few minutes until the golden crumbs become very fine, or leave them coarse for a panko-style crispy breadcrumb.

Transfer to a jar and keep on the shelf for up to 6 months.

POTTED MEATS

SERVES 4

When you have had a roast at the weekend – what to do with leftover meat? I give my cooked meats a shelf life of five days from the day of cooking, so if meat was cooked on Sunday it will be fit to eat until Thursday, if kept chilled.

Potting your leftover meat extends its shelf life from five days to two weeks and the technique has been used for centuries. When I was a child many butchers sold potted meats – obviously their way of avoiding waste. This recipe dates back to 1860 but it is now twenty-first-century 'super fast' and easy thanks to electric food processors rather than the pestle and mortar used back in the day. I adored this as a child (and still do) – great on toast, to take on picnics and fantastic on fresh crusty bread.

Full of flavour, it makes excellent use of leftover roasted meat. Use any cold meat, though it must be lean – I used beef, though this recipe is perfect with ham, turkey, chicken, game, etc. Adjust the recipe to suit the leftover chilled cooked meat that you have.

170g cooked lean roast beef (or other cooked meat)

140g room-temperature butter, cut into small cubes

½ tsp ground mace

½ tsp freshly grated nutmeg (about ¼ nutmeg)

¼ tsp cayenne pepper

You will need:

Chopping board and sharp knife

Food processor with small bowl and blade attached

Small pots or ramekins (I used 4 x 80ml pots)

Teaspoon

Small saucepan

Small jug

Start by cutting the beef (or cooked meat) into small 1cm (½ inch) dice, remove any fat or sinew and place in the small bowl of a food processor with the blade attached. Blitz until the meat has formed a crumb then, with the motor running, add 35g of the butter, a little at a time, then add the spices and continue with 35g more of the butter. After just a few minutes the meat will form a smooth, solid ball. Taste and add more spice if required, though I think it is just right.

Transfer to the pots, allowing 1cm (½ inch) of headroom. Push well down and smooth the surface. I find the back of a teaspoon is the easiest way to do this. To preserve the potted meat it is necessary to cover each pot in a thin layer of clarified butter. In a small saucepan over a low heat melt the remaining 70g butter. Once it is liquid, pour it into a small jug, leaving behind the solids at the bottom of the pan.

Once this clarified butter has cooled to room temperature but is still liquid, pour it over the potted meat, then allow to set and refrigerate until required.

Potted meat will be good to eat for at least two weeks – the layer of butter protects the food from contamination.

FISHCAKES

MAKES 6-8

Leftover mash is a gift and I regularly make more mashed potato than I need, knowing I can put together another meal within the next day or two to use up the excess. The following quick and easy recipe is regularly on the menu – coated in the home-made Golden Breadcrumbs (page 14) and sprayed with our home-blended Spray Oil (page 216).

These no-fuss fishcakes can be sprayed with oil then grilled, oven-baked, air-fried or shallow-fried and served up as a quick lunch or a main meal. I like to serve them alongside a warm Minted Pea Puree (page 20) and maybe a small salad.

You can use fresh or cooked fish here – tinned fish is also very good, as it has high levels of valuable omega-3 fatty acids which are important for overall health and wellbeing, and rich in protein and low in fat to make a healthy meal option that is not expensive. I've added some grated lemon zest, but if you don't have a lemon, don't worry – I forgot to add it one time and the fishcakes were still delicious. This recipe is much better than supermarket equivalents. I often freeze a batch of fishcakes to be either fried, oven-cooked or air-fried quickly when I am stuck for a meal idea.

300g cooked cold
    mashed potato
200g cooked skinless
    salmon fillet, smoked
    mackerel, or 200g tin of
    salmon, tuna or sardines
    in oil or brine, drained
1 tbsp capers (optional)
2 tbsp chopped fresh
    parsley or tarragon,
    or use 1 tbsp dried
    mixed herbs
Finely grated zest
    of 1 lemon
2 spring onions,
    finely chopped
2 tbsp plain flour
1 large egg, beaten
2–3 tbsp Golden
    Breadcrumbs (page 14)
2–3 tbsp vegetable oil
    or sunflower oil, or
    Spray Oil (page 216),
    for frying
Salt and pepper, to taste

To save on washing up I tend to mix all the ingredients together in the pan or bowl that contains the leftover mash. Add the fish to the mash, plenty of seasoning, the capers, if using, herbs, lemon zest and finely chopped spring onions. Mix together well using a fork.

Divide the mixture into 6 or 8 even-sized pieces either by moulding using your hands or less messy is a handy ice cream scoop. Roll the balls in the flour and use your hands to flatten to about 2.5cm (1 inch) thick.

Pop the cakes onto a plate and into the freezer for 15–20 minutes to firm up. Meanwhile, add the beaten egg to one bowl, then add the fine breadcrumbs to the other.

Once the cakes have firmed up in the freezer and can be handled easily, dip them one by one first into the beaten egg, coating the top and bottom and sides, then roll in the dry breadcrumbs. Transfer them back to the plate. I use just one hand – then if I need more breadcrumbs I can top them up without having to abandon the job and wash my hands.

Recipe continued overleaf

You will need:
Zester
Digital weighing scales
Mixing bowl
Fork
Ice-cream scoop
    (optional)
3 bowls – 1 for flour,
    1 for egg, 1 for
    breadcrumbs
Plate
Frying pan, air fryer
    or baking sheet

Once each cake is coated, pop the plate into the fridge until ready to cook, or freeze to use later.

To cook, heat the oil in a large frying pan until hot but not smoking then fry three cakes at a time for 5 minutes on each side until golden and crisp. Turn each one only once – don't be tempted to keep flipping them over because they can easily break. Drain on kitchen paper and keep warm while you cook the rest. Serve with salad or the minted pea puree below.

Alternatively, cook in the air fryer – give each fishcake a light spray of oil, then air-fry for 15 minutes until hot and golden brown, or cook for 20 minutes from frozen.

To oven-bake, spray each fishcake with oil then transfer to a preheated baking sheet and cook for 25 minutes (30 minutes from frozen) in an oven set to 180°C/160°C fan/350°F/gas 4, turning once.

MINTED PEA PUREE

SERVES 4

This works very well with the Fishcakes (page 19 and above) and I serve it warm.

200g frozen peas
15g Mint Sauce
    (page 237) or use
    ready-made
50ml water
Pinch of salt
20g butter

You will need:
Digital weighing scales
Microwave-proof bowl,
    or small saucepan
Hand-held electric
    blender

Place all of the ingredients into a bowl and microwave on High for 2–3 minutes, or until the peas are hot and cooked through. Alternatively, cook on the hob in a small saucepan over a low heat until the peas are soft and the butter melted.

Blitz with the hand-held electric blender until a rough, thick pouring consistency is achieved and serve along with the fishcakes.

TURKEY POT PIES

MAKES 6

I decided to include this recipe because these pies have become a real hit and no more do I groan at the thought of leftover turkey. Roast turkey is my traditional Christmas roast and cold turkey served up on Boxing Day with pickles and chips is a tradition in our house too. I make a stock with the carcass (using the same method as the chicken stock on page 140), yet there is still leftover meat and, to be brutally honest, I can't face it any more.

There are many recipes trying to persuade us to use up our leftover turkey this way or that – turkey curry, turkey stew, turkey soup – and having tried them all I am underwhelmed. My favourite newest addition, however, is my Turkey Pot Pie – prepped after Christmas, frozen unbaked and then a welcome one-pot individual serving at the end of January and into February when the weather is cold, Christmas is a distant memory and turkey can come back onto the menu.

Easy to make, freeze, then cook from frozen – a comfort meal in a pot!

1 tbsp oil
1 tbsp butter
1 onion, finely chopped
2 celery sticks,
    finely diced
2 spring onions,
    finely diced
2 carrots, finely diced
1 tbsp dried mixed herbs
1 tbsp dried tarragon
2 tbsp plain flour
550ml stock (page 140)
150ml cream (double,
    single, whipping or
    crème fraîche)
500g cooked turkey,
    cut into cubes
130g frozen peas
Salt and pepper, to taste

For the pastry
450g plain flour, plus
    extra for dusting
Pinch of salt
115g chilled lard,
    cut into cubes
115g chilled butter,
    cut into cubes
1 large egg, beaten

First, make the pastry. Add the flour, salt and cubed chilled fats to the bowl of a food processor with the blade fitted and blitz for about 10 seconds until the mix resembles breadcrumbs. With the motor running, drizzle in 8 tablespoons of cold water and leave the machine running long enough until the dough forms into a ball.

Take the dough from the bowl, wrap in a beeswax wrap or place on a plate and cover with an upturned bowl, pop into the fridge and leave for 30 minutes to firm up.

In the frying pan, heat the oil and butter then fry the onion for about 10 minutes over a gentle heat until softened and just starting to turn golden. Add the celery, spring onions and carrots to the pan along with the cooked onions. Add all the dried herbs and stir well. Cook for a further 5 minutes then add the flour.

Stir for a minute or so to make sure the veggies get a coating of flour yet the flour doesn't burn onto the base of the pan. Add salt and pepper then the stock, a little at a time, stirring well between each addition. The mixture will bubble and thicken – at this point take from the heat and stir in the cream. Transfer to a large bowl and leave to go completely cold. Once cold, stir through the cooked cubed turkey and frozen peas.

Recipe continued overleaf

You will need:
Digital weighing scales
Food processor with blade
    attached (or mix pastry
    by hand)
Measuring spoons
Beeswax wrap or
    plate and bowl,
    for resting pastry
Frying pan
Wooden spoon
Large bowl
Rolling pin
6 ovenproof soup bowls,
    large ramekins or even
    over-sized mugs or cups
Knife
Pastry brush
Freezer bags
Baking sheet

Take the pastry from the fridge and divide into six pieces. Roll each piece out onto a lightly floured surface to about the thickness of a £1 coin, then use the rim of the ovenproof pie dish you will be using as a guide and the blade of a knife to cut around the pastry.

Divide the cold filling evenly among the six pots then top off with a circle of pastry – easing it onto the filling but not pressing down too firmly. Brush the top of each pie with the beaten egg, make a couple of air holes in the pastry and then freeze. Once completely frozen, pop into freezer bags and freeze for up to 3 months.

When ready to cook, preheat the oven to 200°C/180°C fan/ 400°F/gas 6 with a baking sheet inside.

Pop the frozen pies onto the sheet and bake for 1 hour, until dark golden, hot and bubbling at the sides. Allow to stand for 10 minutes before serving. A pot pie is a meal in itself, though add potatoes and extra vegetables as a side dish if you fancy!

CURRIED HAM CROQUETTES

MAKES 10

Using leftover mash, these went down an absolute storm with quick Fridge-Pickled Cucumbers & Onions (page 232) and made a very satisfying quick and easy meal. Or serve with a salad. Very little meat is needed for this recipe – the ingredients may seem underwhelming but the taste is amazing. You can air-fry, shallow-fry or oven-bake these for a crispy crumb.

60g cooked ham
1 small shallot or onion
1 tbsp dried mixed herbs
    or 2 tbsp chopped
    fresh (rosemary, mint,
    thyme, parsley)
350g cold mashed potato
1 tbsp cornflour
1 tbsp curry powder
3–4 tbsp Golden
    Breadcrumbs (page 14)
Spray Oil (page 216)
    or 1–2 tbsp oil

You will need:
Digital weighing scales
Measuring spoons
Food processor with
    small bowl and blade
    attached (optional)
    or chopping board
    and knife
Mixing bowl
Fork
Air fryer, frying pan
    or baking sheet

The cooked ham needs to be finely blitzed in a food processor along with the onion and herbs. If making by hand, very finely chop – I have even used a pestle and mortar or end of a rolling pin to mash the chopped ham with the raw onion and herbs.

Once the ham, onion and herbs have formed into a rough paste they can be mixed with the mashed potato, cornflour and curry powder. Mix thoroughly then form into small croquettes about 40–50g each. Form either into balls or cylinders then roll into a small bowl containing the breadcrumbs. I don't bother with the faff of dipping in beaten egg first – the breadcrumbs adhere to the croquette. Chill on a plate until ready to cook.

Spray with oil then air-fry for 10 minutes or shallow-fry with 1–2 tablespoons of oil for 10–12 minutes, turning during cooking, or oven-bake after a spray of oil for 20–25 minutes.

UNIVERSAL COTTAGE PIE

SERVES 4

Cottage pie, made with leftover roast beef or fresh minced beef, and shepherd's pie, made using leftover roast lamb or fresh minced lamb, are those nostalgic family comfort foods. Back in the day, one of the best cottage pies was served as a school dinner – I loved it. There are many recipes to choose from with each chef adding their own personal twist.

I have also seen many 'ready meals' enticing us to the supermarket deals with a photograph showing a delicious-looking cottage pie or shepherd's pie that can be popped straight into the oven in its single-use tray. Again, I am left wondering what unknown extras have to go into it for such a long shelf life.

Try this – it doesn't take long to make from scratch, can be adjusted to suit any palate, made ahead and frozen or simply chilled for up to five days. I call it my 'Universal Cottage Pie', as it can be adjusted to be gluten-free, dairy-free, vegan or vegetarian, and is very tasty.

Even though I eat meat, I have reduced my meat intake and will bulk out many a dish using lentils. Cooked well, in stock, they are very flavoursome and tender and very good for you. You'll never know you're not eating minced beef. The first time I made this recipe I used 200g leftover tinned corned beef that had been kicking around in the fridge for a few days but you can use any leftover finely chopped roasted meat. I realise that corned beef is considered to be an ultra-processed food nowadays, but, just like bacon and ham, I do like it from time to time. I consider myself 'flexitarian' – I enjoy most foods, though I am mindful of the pitfalls and will steer towards 'healthy'.

160g green lentils
  or Puy lentils
500ml vegetable
  or chicken stock
4 tbsp oil, butter or lard
2 large onions,
  finely chopped
200g lean leftover
  cooked beef or lamb
  chopped up very
  small or blitzed briefly
  in a food processor
  (meat version)
200g mushrooms
  (vegan version)
2 celery sticks,
  finely diced
2–3 carrots, finely diced

Place the lentils into a metal sieve and rinse under the cold tap, then transfer to a saucepan, add the stock and bring to the boil. Cover and simmer for 30 minutes until the lentils are tender and have absorbed most of the stock. Set aside.

In another saucepan, heat the oil, butter or lard and fry the onions over a low heat for 10 minutes. Add your chopped meat to the pan along with the celery and carrots and add in a pinch each of salt and pepper, and the herbs and nutmeg. For the vegan version, leave out the meat and add the mushrooms instead. Give it a good stir, put the lid on and cook for 15–20 minutes on the lowest heat until the carrots are tender.

Recipe continued overleaf

2 tbsp dried mixed herbs,
   or 4 tbsp chopped
   fresh parsley
1 tsp ground nutmeg
2 tbsp flour, gluten-free
   flour or cornflour
300ml water
900g floury potatoes
   (peeled weight), cut
   into even-sized chunks
Butter or vegan
   alternative
Milk (dairy or non-dairy)
Cheddar cheese,
   Parmesan or vegan
   alternative, grated
   (optional)
Salt and pepper

You will need:
Digital weighing scales
Measuring jug
Metal sieve
3 x saucepans with lids
Chopping board
Knife
Food processor (optional)
Wooden spoon
Family-sized pie dish,
   or make 4 individual
   pies in ovenproof soup
   bowls (I prefer this – we
   eat two and freeze two)
Colander
Potato masher
Fork
Grater

Add the flour, gluten-free flour or cornflour, stir well and cook for a minute or two, then add the contents of the pan containing the lentils and any stock, stir well and simmer. As the sauce thickens, add more water, little by little, stirring between each addition until the sauce is thick but not so thick that the spoon doesn't leave a pool of gravy behind. You may or may not need all of the water. Taste and check the seasoning, then take off the heat – transfer to the pie dish or dishes and leave to cool.

Boil the potatoes in water, adding salt if preferred, and once tender, drain and mash until smooth, adding the seasoning plus a little butter and milk to taste.

Cover the cooked filling with the mashed potato, starting at the outside of the dish(es) then working inwards. Smooth with a fork then add a grating of cheese, Parmesan, or vegan alternative (if using).

Chill or freeze then bake in the oven at 200°C/180°C fan/ 400°F/gas 6 for 25–30 minutes until the potato is golden and the filling is bubbling. Serve with a green vegetable.

COURGETTE CANNELLONI

SERVES 8

For those 'grow your own food' readers, I decided to throw in this recipe as a way to tackle the courgette plant that has seemingly taken over the veggie plot overnight. How did you never see this monster before? I swear they grow faster when you're not at home to keep an eye on them.

Courgettes are an easy crop to grow and will supply endless fruits throughout the summer. I need to tell you this story: I came back from holiday in September to one such courgette. Enormous she was – dark green, not a blemish and bathing in the autumn sunshine. 'I'll have you,' I thought, and immediately cut her from the plant and popped her into the garden shed. This fruit was at least 38cm (15 inches) long and at its widest maybe 15–20cm (6–8 inches). I laid it into my wooden trug on the floor in a dark corner of the shed and there she stayed.

I have no idea why I forgot about this giant but I did until the following January! Can you believe it? This beauty had gathered a layer of dust, which easily washed off, and the courgette was still vivid green, firm and moist inside. I decided to make my 'courgette cannelloni' and my chickens got an out-of-season treat from the trimmings, too!

This recipe is vegetarian – and easy to adapt to vegan – but for meat eaters I like to fill the courgette with my Ragu (see page 121). Low in fat and gluten-free, this tastes delicious with a few chips alongside. Try using a drizzle of sesame oil for frying for a super nutty flavour.

1 very large courgette (see tip overleaf), 300g trimmings, diced
2 tbsp oil (olive oil, rapeseed oil or vegetable oil)
2 large onions, chopped into ½cm (¼ inch) dice
2 red peppers, chopped into 1cm (½ inch) dice
1 large aubergine, chopped into 1cm (½ inch) dice
3 garlic cloves, chopped
1 small glass red wine (optional)
700g Italian passata (page 42)
2 tbsp tomato puree

First, trim the overgrown courgette – keep the trimmings and dice them for the filling. Set the trimmed courgette aside.

Place the casserole dish over a medium heat and add the oil followed by the onions. Give them a good stir then drop the heat to its lowest, put the lid on and leave the onions to sweat for 10 minutes until they become soft and translucent. Take off the lid, turn up the heat then add the diced vegetables and garlic, including the courgette trimmings. Stir and allow the vegetables to brown slightly. This browning of the edges of the vegetables will give extra flavour to the finished dish. Turn down the heat then add the wine, if using, and allow this to bubble and deglaze the base of the pan. If not using the wine move on to the next stage and simply add the passata, tomato puree, herbs, olives, capers and 1 teaspoon each of salt and pepper. Cook over a low heat, uncovered, for 15 minutes until the vegetables are tender and the sauce is thick. Taste and check the seasoning, adding more salt and pepper if necessary. Set aside and allow to cool.

Recipe continued overleaf

3 tbsp chopped mixed fresh
    herbs (basil, oregano,
    parsley, thyme), or 1½
    tbsp mixed dried herbs
2 tbsp chopped black olives
2 tbsp capers, chopped
Spray Oil (page 216)
Salt and pepper

For the white sauce:
50g butter or vegan butter
50g plain flour, cornflour
    or gluten-free flour
400ml milk (or non-
    dairy milk)
1 tsp freshly grated
    nutmeg
150g grated cheese
    or vegan cheese
Grated Parmesan cheese
    (or vegan alternative)
    for sprinkling over
Salt and white pepper

You will need:
Knife and chopping
    board
Ovenproof casserole dish
    with a well-fitting lid
Wooden spoon
Mandoline or large knife
Large frying pan or skillet
Spatula
A baking dish (or two)
    greased or brushed with
    Lining Paste (page 86).
    This will make a large
    dish – 30 x 20 x 6cm
    (12 x 8 x 2½ inches) or
    two smaller ones – each
    feeding four people
    (one for now and one
    for the freezer) –
    23 x 15 x 6cm
    (9 x 6 x 2½ inches)
Medium saucepan
Hand whisk
Grater

Meanwhile, make the cannelloni. Cut the trimmed courgette into long slices lengthways – a mandoline will give perfect slices if you have one, or use a sharp knife and cut as thinly as you can. Lay on kitchen paper or a clean tea towel and pat dry on both sides. Heat a dry frying pan, or better still a skillet, to piping hot then spray oil onto one side of the courgette slices, fry quickly for a minute or two until the surface is brown, then flip over, fry the other sides and remove to a plate to cool.

Take each cold fried slice of courgette and fill with a couple of tablespoons of cold vegetable ragu sauce (or Meat Ragu, page 121) then roll up and place into the prepared dish. Continue with the filling and rolling until your dish is full and the little rolls are tightly packed. Season with salt and pepper.

To make the white sauce, in a medium saucepan place the butter, flour, milk, nutmeg and a pinch each of salt and white pepper. Stir over a low heat using a small whisk until the butter melts then turn up the heat and stir continually until the sauce thickens. Cook for a further minute with the heat reduced, then add about 100g of the grated cheese. Stir well then pour over the dish of filled courgette strips.

Scatter the remaining cheese over and add a grating of fresh Parmesan, if desired.

Bake at 200°C/180°C fan/400°F/gas 6 for 40–50 minutes until dark golden brown and bubbling. Leave to stand for 10 minutes before serving.

This can also be frozen once prepared, then cooked from frozen – but allow 1 hour to 1 hour 15 minutes in the oven.

TIP
A very large courgette, about 30cm (12 inches) long and 10cm (4 inches) wide, ends trimmed, cut in half, will yield around 20 slices – sufficient to make this recipe. Of course, you can use regular cannelloni tubes instead – gluten-free or vegan – if you like.

TIP
For the vegetable ragu – you may not need all of this sauce but any surplus can be frozen and served as ratatouille. Chop the vegetables really small for maximum flavour.

ALL-VEGGIE CURRY

SERVES 4

This recipe even surprised me! Faced with a selection of root veggies that needed to be used up – plentiful greens from the garden, a couple of onions, garlic and a tin of tomatoes – this plate of food absolutely hit the spot. It's super tasty and ready for the table in just over half an hour.

For those with a big appetite, I would say serve with boiled rice, but for me the curry on its own (as it has potatoes included) was perfect.

4 tbsp oil of choice
   and a knob of butter
   (vegans use just oil)
2 large onions,
   thinly sliced
4 garlic cloves, chopped
600g root vegetables
   (peeled weight) –
   I used swede, potatoes
   and carrot, cut into
   2cm (¾ inch) dice
2 tbsp medium curry
   powder
2 tsp cumin seeds
½ tsp each of salt
   and pepper
250ml cold water
300g spinach, chard, kale
   or wild garlic (trimmed
   weight), stalks removed
   and leaves roughly torn
1 tbsp cornflour and
   2 tbsp cold water
   mixed to a paste
400g tin of chopped
   tomatoes
1 tbsp tomato puree

You will need:
Chopping board and knife
Measuring spoons
2 large saucepans, both
   with well-fitting lids
Wooden spoon
Cup or small jug for
   cornflour mix

In a large saucepan heat 3 tablespoons of the oil and the butter, add three-quarters of the onions, stir well to separate the slices then fry slowly for 10 minutes until the onions have softened. Add the garlic to the pan along with the diced root vegetables. Add the curry powder and cumin seeds, salt and pepper and stir well. Fry gently for 5 minutes, stirring from time to time until all the veggies are coated with the spices. Pour over the cold water and stir, add the lid and simmer for 25 minutes until the vegetables are very tender.

In the meantime, heat the remaining tablespoon of oil in the other pan, add the remaining onion and fry gently for 5 minutes. Add the washed greens – it is absolutely fine if the leaves are still wet – stir, pop the lid on and cook gently for 10–15 minutes, stirring from time to time so that they don't catch and burn on the bottom of the pan. The leaves will reduce considerably – what was a pan full to the brim with greens will have reduced to a dark delicious-looking leafy sauce. Remove from the heat and set aside.

Once the pan of root vegetables are cooked, pour in the cornflour paste and stir to slightly thicken, then add the tin of tomatoes, tomato puree and finally the cooked greens. Stir well, taste and adjust the seasoning if you think necessary.

Serve with boiled rice and a garnish of fresh coriander leaves and sliced fresh mild red chilli if you have it.

RASPBERRY & ALMOND BREAD & BUTTER PUDDING

SERVES 4

A bread and butter pudding is a great way to use up stale bread, but so often there is not quite enough leftover bread or maybe too much! To solve this, as stale bread will freeze, I bag it up until there is enough to make a pudding.

This recipe serves four, but it can be easily scaled up. I don't bother cutting off the crusts here, and I use frozen berries, with the sugar cut to a minimum. Baking this pudding in a bain marie ensures the sides of the pudding don't burn and the dish is just light and delicious, with a crisp almond-crusted top. Try it!

200g stale bread
20g butter
20g sugar
60g frozen raspberries
2 large eggs
140ml milk
40ml single or
    double cream
    (or use more milk)
½ tsp almond extract
1 tbsp flaked almonds

You will need:
Pudding dish or tin,
    greased or brushed with
    Lining Paste (page 86)
    – my oval one measures
    20 x 15 x 5cm (8 x 6 x
    2 inches)
Pastry brush
Digital weighing scales
Measuring spoons
Bread board
Bread knife
Rolling pin
Freezer bag
Measuring jug
Fork
Roasting tin large
    enough to contain
    the pudding dish

Lightly grease the pudding dish or brush with lining paste. Slice the bread thinly then butter one side of each slice. Cut the bread into small triangles and place one layer, butter-side down, into the pudding dish so that the base is covered. Sprinkle over a teaspoon of the sugar.

Crush the frozen raspberries to a crumb using the end of a rolling pin. This can be done easily if the weighed-out frozen berries are placed in a freezer bag first. Scatter over half of the berry crumbs then cover with another layer of buttered bread – butter-side up. Scatter over another teaspoon of sugar and the rest of the berries.

In the measuring jug, combine the eggs, milk, cream and almond extract, beating with a fork. Pour the mixture over the bread in the dish, add any remaining sugar and a sprinkle of flaked almonds. Leave for about 1 hour – during this time the bread will soak up the liquid. This pudding will sit happily in the fridge for several hours until you are ready to bake.

When ready to bake, preheat the oven to 200°C/180°C fan/400°F/gas 6.

Place the prepared pudding into the roasting tin, then boil a kettle of water and carefully pour around the outside of the pudding into the roasting tin. The water needs to come about 2.5cm (1 inch) up the side of the dish. Bake for 35–40 minutes until the pudding is risen and golden.

GLUTEN-FREE BREAD & BUTTER PUDDING

SERVES 6-8

When testing the Gluten-Free Loaf on page 85, I have to say the earlier versions definitely gave me the run around, resulting in an oversupply of slightly substandard white bread. Mindful that the ingredients that I had used and the bread produced was not only costly but perfectly edible, I knew that if I popped them into the freezer they would probably never again see the light of day, so instead I put together this delicious bread and butter pudding.

I have included a few ingredient switches so that you can pretty much make this pudding using whatever you have in the fridge, from the fruit bowl or on the shelf. It uses minimal extra fat because there is fat in the bread (from the mayonnaise), and the refined sugar can be substituted with honey or maple syrup.

1 tsp mixed spice, ground cinnamon, nutmeg, almond or Vanilla Extract (page 213)

60g mixed dried fruits and peel, or use finely diced fresh apple, pear, dried apricots (chopped) or small frozen fruits (try crushed frozen raspberries or blackberries)

30g butter

12 thin slices of gluten-free bread (page 85)

30g sugar, honey or maple syrup

Finely grated zest of 1 lemon

3 large eggs

300ml milk (dairy or non-dairy)

1 tbsp demerara or granulated sugar

Start by buttering your pie dish or simply brush with gluten-free lining paste then set aside.

In a small bowl sprinkle the spices/flavourings over the chosen fruits and give a good stir. For example, cinnamon works well with apple, mixed spice with the dried fruits, nutmeg with apricots, almond extract with raspberries and vanilla extract with blackberries.

Butter the bread very thinly on one side – don't worry if there isn't enough to cover all of the slices – there is already fat in the bread. Place the first layer of bread butter-side down into the dish or tin – use about a third of the bread. Sprinkle over one half of the fruit and flavour mix, add half of the sugar or honey/maple syrup and a grating of lemon zest. Layer over more bread (another third) followed by the rest of the fruit, flavours and sugar/honey. Finish with a layer of bread, butter-side down.

In the jug, beat the eggs with the milk. Stir everything together well then pour over the bread in the tin/dish, allowing it to run down between cracks and crevices.

Note: Once the pudding has been prepared to this stage it can be popped into the fridge for several hours or frozen.

Recipe continued overleaf

A pie dish or tin, greased
  or brushed with
  Gluten-Free Lining
  Paste (page 86) –
  mine measures
  26 x 20 x 2.5cm
  (10 x 8 x 1 inch)
Digital weighing scales
Small bowl
Spoon
Butter knife
Zester
Measuring jug
Fork
A roasting tin deep and
  large enough to hold
  the pudding tin or dish
Measuring spoon

TIP
To make this not gluten-
free, simply substitute
the 12 slices of gluten-
free bread for 6 slices
of normal wheat bread.

TIP
If you have any dregs of
cream that need using up,
you can use this instead of
(or in combination with)
the milk.

To bake from frozen I first thaw overnight in the fridge.

Preheat the oven to 210°C/190°C fan/425°F/gas 7 and bring a large kettle of water to the boil.

Place the pudding into the roasting tin then pour enough boiling water into the tin to come about halfway up the sides of the dish. Finish the pudding with a sprinkle of granulated or demerara sugar over the top, to give it a crunchy crust, then bake for 30–35 minutes or until the pudding is risen and golden brown on the top.

Take from the water bath and serve warm with a little cream, ice cream or custard.

TIP
Baking in a bain marie (water bath) ensures the pudding doesn't burn or bake hard inside the dish/tin. You will have a light, fluffy bread and butter pudding that the family will love made from simple yet wholesome ingredients.

OFFCUTS PUDDING

SERVES 6

I devised this simple recipe one time after I had made a two-tier christening cake and each cake had three layers. Those readers familiar with making large cakes for stacking know that they must be level. Each cake often needs to be trimmed to remove the slightest dome and each layer needs to be the same thickness.

When I made this cake, after the necessary trimming I was left with no less than 250g of cake offcuts. Even though I would nibble a few and I could have frozen them (but in reality would probably forget about them), I decided instead to made a quick pudding, sufficient to feed 6 people, and I even surprised myself – it was so good, light and fruity.

250g cake offcuts or stale cake (I had a mix of vanilla and lemon sponge)

1 orange

3 sticks rhubarb (about 600g) or use any seasonal fruits (apples, raspberries, plums or frozen fruits)

1 tsp ground ginger (or try cinnamon with apple)

2 large eggs

200ml cream or milk, or mixture of both

1–2 tsp demerara sugar, for sprinkling

You will need:
Large plate
Zester
Chopping board and knife
Baking dish – mine measures 23cm x 16cm x 5cm (9 x 6 x 2 inches) buttered well or brushed with Lining Paste (page 86)
Measuring jug
Measuring spoons

Put the cake offcuts onto a large plate and zest the orange over them.

Segment the orange. Cut the top and bottom from the orange then stand it on a flat surface and pare off the skin as close to the fruit as you can, removing the pith – working from the top of the fruit down to the base. Use a sharp knife to cut out each orange segment, leaving behind the tough membrane yet releasing the perfect segment. Once all of the segments have been cut out, squeeze the orange carcass to release further juice over the plate of sponges.

Cut the rhubarb (or fruit of choice) into small pieces.

Using your hands crumble the juice- and zest-soaked sponge into the baking dish, alternating with the fruits of choice. Note there is no additional sugar being added to the ingredients as there is sufficient sweetness in the cake offcuts. Sprinkle over the ginger.

Add the cream/milk mix to the jug – use half and half or all milk or all cream, and crack in the eggs. Beat the eggs and cream together then pour over the cake, fruits and spice in the baking dish. Sprinkle over the demerara sugar to give a crunchy crust.

Bake at 170°C/150°C fan/340°F/gas 4 for 40 minutes until risen and golden. Serve hot with custard, cream or ice cream.

STRAWBERRY-TOP VINEGAR

MAKES 400ML

Summer time and fresh strawberries are gorgeous. I love to make Strawberry-Top Vinegar – or rather it makes itself! Use in any recipe that calls for vinegar or use in the fabulous simple salad dressing below.

Enough strawberry
  tops to fill a jam jar
400ml distilled
  white vinegar

You will need:
500ml jam jar with
  a screw-top lid
Measuring jug
Sieve
Funnel
Paper coffee filter
  or kitchen paper
Attractive clean and
  sterilised (page 231)
  400ml glass vinegar
  or sauce bottle

Place the strawberry tops into the empty jam jar. The more you have, the more flavoured and colourful the vinegar.

Pour over the white vinegar, making sure every leaf and fruit piece is covered. Cover with the lid then leave in a cool place out of direct sunlight for 3–7 days.

When ready to decant your coloured and flavoured vinegar, suspend the sieve over the measuring jug, then pour the contents of the jam jar over. The rich red vinegar will strain into the jug and the strawberry tops can go into the compost.

To remove any trace of fruit, pass the strained vinegar through a filter. Add the funnel to the neck of the bottle to be used, then line the funnel with a paper coffee filter or square of kitchen paper. Pour the vinegar through the paper filter and into the bottle. It will keep for at least 6 weeks.

STRAWBERRY-TOP VINAIGRETTE

SERVES 8-10

Fresh and fruity, this simple vinaigrette, mixed in the jar, is a great addition to summer salads. I like it drizzled over fresh young summer garden vegetables – try it over warm broad beans, peas and baby carrots!

5 tbsp Strawberry-top
  Vinegar (above)
8 tbsp olive oil
1 tsp mustard powder
Pinch of salt and pepper
1–2 tbsp finely chopped
  fresh herbs (chives,
  parsley, basil, coriander)

You will need:
Jam jar with screw-top lid
Measuring spoons

Measure all of the ingredients into the jar, screw on the lid tightly then shake to emulsify.

Taste and adjust the seasoning as required.

Once mixed, the vinaigrette will keep in the fridge for 2–3 days.

TOMATOES

Over the many decades that I have been growing my own food – and especially tomatoes – I have often been told that the trouble is that everything is ready at once. There are only so many tomatoes that can be eaten during August and September and after all that effort, they either are wasted or have to be given away. The shops too have them going cheap, so why go to the bother?

Tomatoes are SO easy to grow (with or without a greenhouse) and it is true, once they begin to ripen it is a job to keep up. However, I rarely need to buy a tin of tomatoes, as I make enough thick tomato passata to keep me going all the year round. I have jars on the pantry shelf to use in pasta sauces, soups, pizzas, stews, curries, lasagnes – in fact, any recipe that would have a tin of tomatoes among its ingredients.

Large beef tomatoes are so proud – I cherish them and often serve in the following ways:

Greenhouse Salad
I think they are delicious sliced and served in what I call my simple 'greenhouse salad'. Room-temperature – or even better sun-warmed and picked fresh – sliced thickly, seasoned with sea salt, drizzled with olive oil and a scattering of greenhouse basil leaves. With some fresh crusty bread alongside, I am in heaven.

Stuffed Tomatoes
These are splendid – they look and taste amazing and manage to tick so many boxes: vegan, vegetarian, low-fat, gluten-free, dairy-free, no refined sugar, and can be grilled, oven-baked or popped into the air fryer. See full recipe opposite.

BAKED STUFFED TOMATOES

MAKES 6

A great summer dish that can easily be scaled up to serve a crowd. If you want to get ahead you can fill your tomatoes, pop the lids on then chill in the fridge for 8 hours before cooking. These are delicious served on their own or to accompany sausages or bacon.

6 large beef tomatoes (each weighing 200g or over) – I like to leave the stalk on
3 tbsp olive oil (or oil of choice)
1 onion, very finely chopped
3 garlic cloves, finely chopped
100g chestnut mushrooms, finely chopped
1 tsp ground nutmeg
1 tsp dried mixed herbs
100g easy-cook rice
2 tsp tomato puree
100ml boiling water
4 tbsp chopped fresh parsley, basil and/ or mint
4 tbsp chopped fresh chives or 2 spring onions, finely chopped
Salt and pepper

You will need:
Digital weighing scales
Chopping board and vegetable knife
Teaspoon or a grapefruit knife if you have one
Small bowl
Baking tray or plate
Measuring spoons
Medium saucepan with lid
Wooden spoon

Using a sharp vegetable knife, slice the tops from your tomatoes, about 1.5cm (½ inch) from the top. Set the tops of the tomato, with the stalk still attached, to one side as these will become the 'lids' once stuffed. Use a teaspoon (or the grapefruit knife) to scoop out the juice, seeds and pulp of the tomato and place this in a bowl. Place the scooped-out beauties onto a plate or baking tray. Chop the pulp of the tomato a little – the large cores are quite thick so cut these into smaller pieces to ensure they cook through later.

In a medium saucepan heat 2 tablespoons of the oil then fry the onion over a medium heat for about 10 minutes until softened. Add the garlic and chopped mushrooms and fry for a few minutes more. Add the nutmeg, dried herbs and rice. Give a good stir then add the tomato pulp, tomato puree and the boiling water. Bring to a gentle simmer, put a lid on the pan, turn the heat down to its lowest setting and cook for 15 minutes.

Take from the heat and give a good stir. The rice will have cooked and absorbed the liquid. Sir in the fresh herbs, then taste and add seasoning as required. Leave to cool.

Once cooled enough to handle, fill your tomatoes right to the top, packing the rice down using the back of the teaspoon as you go, then top off with the 'lids'. Drizzle over the remaining oil and either bake in the oven on the baking tray for 30 minutes at 180°C/160°C fan/350°F/gas 4, grill under a medium preheated grill on the baking tray for 20 minutes or air-fry in the air fryer basket for 12–15 minutes at 200°C until the tomatoes are tender and the skins are just beginning to caramelise.

PASSATA

MAKES 6 450G (1LB) JARS

This is a great recipe for using up those gluts of split tomatoes, misshapen or wonky fruits and, even if you don't have the time to make it when the tomatoes are ripe (maybe you are going on holiday), the tomatoes can be popped into the freezer and the sauce made later when you have the time.

2kg ripe tomatoes
3 tbsp olive oil
   or rapeseed oil
2 onions, chopped
4 garlic cloves, chopped
1½ tbsp dried
   mixed herbs
1 tsp sugar
Salt and pepper

You will need:
Digital weighing scales
Measuring spoons
Sharp knife
Large heatproof bowl
Very large saucepan
   or casserole dish
Large wooden spoon
Stick blender
6 x 450g (1lb) glass jars
   with screwtop lids
Tea towel or cloth

Start by skinning the larger tomatoes (it is not essential on very small ones). Skinning may seem a bit tedious with so many tomatoes, but it is worth it because the skins are tough and can refuse to break down, resulting in sharp shards spoiling the finished sauce. I decided one year to skip this step, only to find the unpleasant 'fish-bone'-type feeling when I was eating my home-made pasta sauce. From then on I have always skinned tomatoes.

To skin, slit each tomato at its base with a sharp knife to make a cross. Place the tomatoes in a large heatproof bowl then pour boiling water over. Leave for about 3–4 minutes then pour off the water. When the tomatoes are cool enough to handle, starting at the base of the tomato where you have made the cross, carefully peel off the skins. They should come off easily, especially if the tomatoes are really ripe. Once all the tomatoes are skinned, set aside the skins (see Tip) and the skinned tomatoes.

In a very large saucepan or casserole dish heat the oil, then add the onions and fry gently for about 10 minutes until softened. Add the garlic, dried herbs and sugar, stir well, then add a pinch each of salt and pepper and the tomatoes. I tend to cut the tomatoes in half as I add them to the dish to help release the juices. Turn up the heat, stir well and bring everything to the boil. Once bubbling away nicely, turn down the heat, maintaining a gentle simmer, and leave uncovered for 2 hours. Stir occasionally with the large wooden spoon.

After the cooking time your tomatoes will have reduced down and thickened. I like a really smooth tomato sauce, so I then give it a quick blitz with a stick blender. Taste for seasoning then leave to cool in the dish before storing.

Those skins don't go to waste, by the way, they are washed and then dried out in the sun, in a dehydrator, or a low oven until crispy, then blitzed to a fine powder and packed into a clean, used spice jar to use as a tomato seasoning! You can also do this with washed onion and garlic skins, and dried red pepper skins can be transformed into your own home-made paprika!

This passata will freeze for a year (stored in plastic tubs or boxes), but if you are short of freezer space and indeed if you have lots of tomatoes, the sauce can be transferred into jars while still hot. The glass jars and lids need to be sterilised (see page 231).

Fill the jars with the hot sauce, then screw on the lids and place in a large saucepan with the jars resting on a small cloth so that they don't bang together. Fill the pan with water so that it completely covers the sealed jars. Bring to the boil and simmer for 20 minutes without a lid on. After that time turn off the heat, cover with a lid and leave the jars of sauce to stand for 40 minutes. This method will create a vacuum seal inside the jar. Remove from the water, check to make sure the lids are screwed on tight, then label and store in a cool place.

EGG WHITES

When it comes to leftovers, egg whites come high on the list. So often egg yolks are used for a recipe but what to do with the whites? And just one egg white is so annoying and pretty useless. So I freeze mine – I pop the white into a silicone tea-cake mould, freeze, then store the small frozen domes individually in a freezer box. Once I have a few I can then think about making something with them. Meringues are the obvious choice, but for those wanting something different, how about cake, buns or marshmallows?

COCONUT & PASSION FRUIT ANGEL CAKES

MAKES 12 SMALL CAKES OR 1 15CM (6 INCH) SANDWICH CAKE

These cakes use just three leftover whites or pre-frozen ones (defrosted for an hour or so), and the flavours here are delicious.

125g soft margarine or
  room-temperature
  butter
180g caster sugar
150ml milk
½ tsp Vanilla Extract
  (page 213)
150g plain flour
½ tsp baking powder
50g desiccated coconut
3 egg whites

For the passion fruit curd
4 passion fruits
2 large eggs
75g sugar (caster
  or granulated)
50g room-temperature
  butter

To complete the frosting:
200ml double cream
10g icing sugar

You will need:
Digital weighing scales
Measuring spoons
Chopping board
  and knife
Teaspoon
Metal sieve
3 mixing bowls
Medium saucepan
Heatproof or
  microwave-safe jug
Hand-held electric whisk
Metal spoon

Start by making the passion fruit curd. First, extract the juice from the passion fruit. Cut the fruits in half then, using a teaspoon, scrape out the seeds into a metal sieve set over a small bowl. Rub the pulp and seeds to release the juice and set aside. Keep the seeds for decoration later.

Place the eggs in a medium saucepan, beat well, then add all the other ingredients for the curd. Stir constantly over a low heat until the butter has melted and the sugar has dissolved, then increase the heat and stir continuously until the curd thickens. Transfer to a heatproof jug or bowl and allow to cool completely.

Alternatively, this can be made in the microwave. Place the eggs in a non-metal, microwave-safe jug, beat well then add the sugar, soft butter and juice. Microwave on High in three or four 20-second bursts, stirring between each. Once the curd is thickened and smooth, cover and allow to cool completely.

To make the sponge, whisk together the margarine (or butter) and sugar in a bowl with the hand-held electric whisk until the mixture is light and fluffy. I then add about one-quarter of the milk plus the vanilla and about one-quarter of the flour, sifted in with the baking powder, and keep mixing until everything is incorporated. Repeat until all the flour and milk have been added and the mixture is smooth, then fold in the coconut and set aside.

In a separate bowl and with clean whisks (any grease or fat in the bowl or on the whisk will prevent the egg whites whisking to their full potential), whisk the egg whites until they are standing in soft peaks and increased in size. Fold this light and airy meringue into the bowl of creamed batter.

Recipe continued overleaf

12-hole muffin tin
  with 12 paper cases
  or 2 x 15cm (6 inch)
  sandwich tins, bases
  lined and brushed with
  Lining Paste (page 86)
Cooling rack
Piping bag

To do this, fold in one spoonful which will begin to slacken the mixture. Repeat one spoon at a time until the mixture is sufficiently slackened and the rest of the meringue can be folded in easily.

Preheat the oven to 180°C/160°C fan/350°F/gas 4. Divide the mixture evenly among the 12 muffin cases or the two tins then bake for 18–20 minutes (25 minutes for the larger cakes) until the cakes are risen, golden and firm to the touch – the sponges will be quite pale because of the absence of the egg yolk. Remove from the oven and allow to cool in the tin on a cooling rack.

To make the frosting, simply whisk together the double cream and icing sugar until thickened (but not too much!), then fold in the passion fruit curd. Transfer to a piping bag and pipe the cream over the cakes. Finish with a few passion fruit seeds and a dusting of desiccated coconut or icing sugar, if you like.

MARSHMALLOWS

MAKES 36

These pillow-soft bon-bons are very easy to eat and adored by adults and children alike, and are also gluten- and fat-free.

5 gelatine sheets
100g caster sugar
50g liquid glucose
2 egg whites
50g freeze-dried fruit
    powder (flavour of
    choice) or try coffee
    or cocoa powder
1 tsp Vanilla Extract
    (page 213)
1 tbsp cornflour, for
    dusting the tin and the
    finished marshmallows
Oil, for greasing

You will need:
Digital weighing scales
Measuring spoons
500ml jug
Saucepan
Temperature probe
Hand-held electric whisk
Mixing bowl
20cm (8 inch) square cake
    tin lined with baking
    paper then dusted
    with cornflour
Spoon or angled
    palette knife
Sharp knife
Sieve

TIP
You can make many
different fruit flavours
of marshmallows.
Try adding strawberry
powder and ¼ teaspoon
ground cinnamon in
place of vanilla.

Fill the jug with cold water, add the gelatine leaves and leave them to soften. The rigid leaves will become soft and floppy. Leave the gelatine in the cold water until ready to use.

Put the sugar, liquid glucose and 50ml water in a saucepan and dissolve the sugar over a low heat until the mixture is clear. Don't stir, just tilt the pan from side to side until it melts. Once you have a clear liquid, turn up the heat, bring to the boil – pop in your temperature probe and allow it to boil to a temperature of 119°C. This will take about 5 minutes.

When the temperature has reached 114°C, whisk the egg whites in a clean bowl until you have stiff peaks, then with the whisk still running carefully pour over the hot sugar syrup in a slow, steady stream. Continue to whisk until the mixture has cooled to body temperature – about 3–4 minutes. At the end of the whisking period add the fruit powder and the vanilla.

While the mixture is still warm, add the gelatine. My tip here is when you have poured all of the syrup out of the pan, drop the wet and drained gelatine leaves into the warm empty pan. The residual heat will be enough to melt the gelatine into a thick syrup. Pour this into the meringue and continue to mix. You will see the mixture start to thicken. Now you need to stop whisking.

Transfer the mix into the prepared tin and smooth it out with the back of a metal spoon or angled palette knife. Leave to set in a cool place or the fridge for at least 4 hours.

Once the marshmallow is set and feeling firm to the touch, turn it out of the tin and peel back the paper. Using a greased, sharp knife, neaten the edges, then cut into even-sized cubes. I then like to sift over a thin dusting of cornflour to the tops and the bottoms. Store in an airtight tin for up to 3 weeks.

SOUPS, STEWS & CASSEROLES

I am reluctant to write specific recipes in this chapter because
I would like you to feel confident enough to throw in whatever you
have (within reason). Once the home cook gains the confidence to
understand flavour pairings and successful switches, then the skill
set for making great soups and stews knows no boundaries.

SOUPS

Let us start with soups.

Whether a hearty bowl of soup is being served up with fresh bread at lunchtime, as a tasty starter before a main meal or simply in a mug when working outdoors on a cold bleak day, soup is a cheap, easy bowl of food.

There are many tins, packets and ready-made soups available in the supermarket but they will all be loaded with extra additives, salts and sugars to both extend their shelf life and enhance their flavour.

Soups made at home can be frozen into portions and be just as convenient as their ultra-processed equivalents. They are so versatile and can be cooked quickly in a pressure cooker (around 10 minutes), in a slow cooker for 2 hours, on the hob or in the oven if it is on anyway for something else.

Try these delicious recipes with a few swaps of your own thrown in.

MUSHROOM SOUP

SERVES 6

This is a great recipe to use up mushrooms that are looking a bit drab or if you have picked up a half-price bargain at the shops. It is also easily adapted to gluten-free, dairy-free and vegan. This soup freezes well.

75g butter, or vegan
   alternative
1 large red or white onion,
   finely chopped
2–3 garlic cloves, finely
   chopped, or 1 tsp
   garlic granules
350g mushrooms,
   thinly sliced
50g plain or gluten-free
   plain flour (or browned
   flour, page 208)
1 tsp grated nutmeg
   (or ½ tsp ground mace,
   1 tsp dried thyme or
   1 tsp mixed dried herbs)
500ml chicken (page 140)
   or vegetable (page 206)
   stock
500ml whole or semi-
   skimmed milk, or
   plant-based equivalent
1–2 tsp lemon juice
   or 1 tsp vinegar
125ml cream (double,
   single or non-dairy)
Salt and pepper

You will need:
Digital weighing scales
Measuring spoons
Chopping board and knife
Large saucepan with
   well-fitting lid
Wooden spoon
Measuring jug
Hand-held electric blender

Heat the butter or vegan equivalent in a large saucepan. Add the onion to the pan and fry over a low heat steadily for 10 minutes until the onion softens but doesn't colour. Add the garlic and mushrooms to the pan and stir around. Add some salt and pepper, then the flour along with the nutmeg or other flavouring. Stir the flour around in the saucepan continually for a minute or two to allow the flour to cook but not stick and burn on the bottom of the pan.

Pour in a little of the stock and stir into the mushrooms. Once mixed in, continue to add the rest of the stock a little at a time to prevent lumps forming. Turn up the heat until the soup begins to boil, then once bubbling turn the heat down to a simmer, add a lid and cook for 15–20 minutes.

Remove from the heat, take off the lid and use a hand-held electric blender to blitz the soup as smooth as you would like. You may want a creamy smooth soup or a more rustic soup with pieces of mushroom present. Pour in the milk, add the lemon juice or vinegar (for a little acidity) and the cream.

Stir and check the seasoning, adding more salt and pepper if necessary.

Serve immediately or reheat before serving.

CARROT & CORIANDER SOUP

SERVES 6-8

Root vegetables make the most deliciously smooth, hearty soups which need no additional thickening. Carrots are so cheap to buy, so I urge you to get a good bunch and make this colourful gorgeous soup. If you slice your carrots thinly, not only will more flavour be released but the soup will also be done in around 30 minutes. This recipe also has easy gluten-free, dairy-free and vegan swaps. This soup will freeze well too.

15g butter, or vegan
   alternative
1 tbsp oil of choice
   (olive, rapeseed,
   vegetable, avocado, etc.)
1 large onion,
   finely chopped
1 tbsp coriander seeds
500g carrots, peeled
   and thinly sliced
1 garlic clove,
   finely cahopped
1 celery stick, finely
   chopped, or ½ tsp
   celery salt
400ml chicken (page 140)
   or vegetable (page 206)
   stock
80ml double cream,
   single cream or non-
   dairy equivalent,
   to serve (optional)
Salt and pepper

You will need:
Digital weighing scales
Measuring spoons
Chopping board and knife
Large saucepan with
   a well-fitting lid
Wooden spoon
Frying pan
Pestle and mortar or bowl
   and a rolling pin
Measuring jug
Stick blender or liquidiser

In the large saucepan over a low heat melt the butter or vegan equivalent with the oil, add the chopped onion and give it a good stir, then place the lid on and leave to sweat for 8–10 minutes.

While the onion is softening toast the coriander seeds in a dry frying pan. Heat gently until their perfume is released. Remove from the heat and transfer to a pestle and mortar or bowl – don't leave them in the pan any longer, as the residual heat could cause them to burn. Crush the seeds using the pestle and mortar.

Add the carrots, garlic, coriander seed, celery or celery salt and a little salt and pepper to the onion. Give everything a good stir then add the stock. Turn up the heat and once bubbling turn down to a simmer, replace the lid and cook for 15–20 minutes until the thinly sliced carrot is tender.

Take off the heat then blitz with a stick blender or liquidise until smooth, thick and a gorgeous colour. Stir in the cream, if using, and check the seasoning. Serve hot.

TIPS
Carrot soup on its own with no flavour pairing is delicious, simply garnished with some chopped parsley, but you can add a couple of ingredients for variety. For Carrot and Orange soup, instead of the coriander add the zest and juice of 1 orange, and for Carrot and Ginger soup, use 2 tbsp grated fresh ginger instead of coriander.

STEWS & CASSEROLES

Many many years ago I attended a French cookery course and was taught how to make classic Boeuf Bourguignon – and it took all of three days! The meat and vegetables had to be marinated in red wine for 24 hours, then drained, dried and fried. Then there was a long, slow cooking followed by removing the meat and vegetables and reducing the sauce before adding back the meat and vegetables. The onions and mushrooms were cooked separately, too, then stirred in right at the end. The whole lot was then left for a day and served the next. It tasted delicious, though I have to say, there was no marked difference to my simpler 'all-in-one' version that you'll find on the next page!

'ALL-IN-ONE' BEEF BOURGUIGNON

SERVES 4–6

Beef Bourguignon – wholesome, hearty and this version is very easy to make. If you prefer to use stewing beef, avoid finely diced meat, buy a large piece and cut it into 5cm (2 inch) chunks. Three to four pieces, along with onions, mushrooms and carrots make up a hearty portion. This recipe can be easily scaled up to serve a crowd – 4kg meat cooked in two large casserole dishes will easily serve 16 people – and it freezes well too. Serve with mashed potatoes and a green vegetable.

15g dripping, lard or oil
100g bacon lardons
1 large onion,
    finely chopped
40g fresh parsley,
    stalks chopped,
    leaves for garnish
1 tbsp dried mixed herbs
1kg shin or stewing beef
1 tsp each salt and black
    pepper, plus extra
1 heaped tbsp browned
    (page 208) flour, plain
    flour or cornflour
4–5 garlic cloves,
    finely chopped
1 tsp mustard
1 tbsp brown sugar
2 celery sticks, sliced
3 medium carrots, cut into
    5cm (2 inch) chunks
150g chestnut mushrooms,
    cut in half
8 shallots, peeled
200ml beef stock
100ml red wine

You will need:
Digital weighing scales
Chopping board
    and knife
Measuring jug
Measuring spoons
Large casserole dish
    with a well-fitting lid
Wooden spoon

Heat the fat or oil in the ovenproof casserole dish or multi-cooker then add the bacon, onion, parsley stalks and dried herbs. Stir well with a wooden spoon and fry gently for 10 minutes or until the bacon is just starting to colour and the onions are softened.

Cut the meat into 5cm (2 inch) chunks and add to the dish with the salt and pepper, flour, garlic, mustard and brown sugar. Turn up the heat and stir continuously until the meat browns and has a coating of flour and flavours.

Lower the heat, then add the celery, carrots, mushrooms and shallots and stir well. Pour in the stock and wine, stir well then cook as follows. Cook on low in the slow cooker for 10–12 hours, or put the lid on the casserole dish and cook in the bottom (simmering) oven of the Aga for 12 hours (I left mine as long as 16 hours and it was delicious), or the oven at 130°C/110°C fan/225°F/gas ¼ for 5–6 hours.

After the cooking time, remove the lid and taste the sauce, adding more seasoning if necessary. The meat should be very tender and the sauce just the right consistency – coating the meat and vegetables but also giving a smooth pool of sauce. If the sauce is too thick, add hot water. If the sauce is too thin, remove the lid and return to the oven to reduce slightly for half an hour or so, or mix 1 tablespoon of cornflour or plain flour and around 100ml cold water to a thin paste in a cup or small jug and stir this into the hot sauce until thickened.

Leave to go completely cold and reheat the next day or serve straight away. Sprinkle over chopped fresh parsley leaves to serve, if you like.

BEEF IN BEER

SERVES 4

This simple beef stew tastes unbelievably good and is derived from a dish I once tasted while in France – carbonnade flamande. It's a real crowd-pleaser and so easy to make.

1kg braising steak,
    cut into large 5–7.5cm
    (2–3 inch) chunks
2 tbsp oil of choice
Large knob of butter
1 large onion or 2 small,
    thinly sliced
4 carrots, cut into 5cm
    (2 inch) chunks
4 juniper berries, crushed,
    or 1 tsp finely chopped
    fresh rosemary
3 large sprigs of thyme
440ml can of dark beer
    (not lager)
400ml water
4 slices of Spiced Bread
    (page 104) or Jamaican-
    style spiced bun
4 tsp English mustard
Salt and pepper

You will need:
Digital weighing scales
Measuring jug
Measuring spoons
Chopping board
    and knife
Large casserole dish
    with a well-fitting lid
Wooden spoon

Season the beef chunks well with salt and pepper. Heat the oil in the casserole dish then fry the beef chunks in small batches until well browned on all sides. I fry about six chunks at a time then once browned transfer to a large plate – adding too much meat to the dish at once will result in the meat turning a grey colour and frothing rather than browning. Once the meat is browned it will leave the pan easily, so there's no need to scrape at it while browning.

Preheat the oven to 160°C/140°C fan/325°F/gas 3.

Once the meat is all browned, transfer to a plate, add the knob of butter to the casserole dish, then stir in the onions. Lower the heat and allow them to caramelise slowly for about 15 minutes.

Add the carrots to the dish along with the juniper berries or rosemary and the thyme. Add the pieces of browned meat back into the dish. Stir well then add the beer and water. Spread each slice of spiced bread with the mustard and lay this over the ingredients, pop the lid on and then place in the oven for a low slow braise for 2½ hours.

At the end of the cooking time, take the casserole from the oven, give it a stir and taste to check the seasoning, though I guess you will need to add nothing at all. It is thick, gorgeous and unbelievably tasty. Serve with chips and peas or potatoes and veg of choice.

30-MINUTE CHICKEN & MUSHROOMS

SERVES 4

This recipe was born one Sunday autumn afternoon. The rain was pouring and the temperature much cooler than of late. I fancied something warm and comforting – but quick! With four boneless, skinless chicken breasts in the fridge and a pack of mushrooms, I thought that was perfect for a seasonal recipe. If you have them, dried mushrooms will add a richness to the flavour. Gluten-free, cooked quickly on the hob and served up on plates in half an hour – yummy! I serve this with boiled potatoes, carrots and a green vegetable.

10g dried mushrooms (optional)
300ml apple juice
20ml malt vinegar
150ml water
½ tsp each of salt, freshly ground black pepper and nutmeg
4 heaped tsp cornflour
4 boneless, skinless chicken breasts
120g chestnut mushrooms, thinly sliced
4 tbsp double cream
4–5 tbsp chopped fresh parsley

You will need:
Digital weighing scales
Measuring spoons
Measuring jug
Chopping board and knife
Small heatproof jug
Large saucepan with a well-fitting lid
Cup or mug
Kitchen tongs
Warm bowl and plate
Wooden spoon

Start by soaking the dried mushrooms, if using. Cut them into 2.5cm (1 inch) pieces if they are large then place in a small heatproof jug. Pour over 100ml boiling water and set aside while you cook the chicken.

In the saucepan add the apple juice, malt vinegar, water, salt, pepper and nutmeg, but do not heat yet. Add the cornflour to a cup or mug then stir in 2–3 tablespoons of the cold apple juice mixture to make a paste and set aside – this will be used to thicken the sauce later. Put the saucepan over a medium heat and bring to the boil. Once boiling, using the kitchen tongs add the chicken breasts to the hot liquid then cover with the lid, turn down to a simmer and cook gently for 15 minutes.

After 15 minutes, use the tongs to lift the chicken out of the hot stock to a warm bowl and cover with a plate. The chicken will be cooked through, but if you are in any doubt pierce the thickest part with the point of a sharp knife – any juices should run clear.

Add the sliced mushrooms and the dried mushrooms plus their soaking liquid (if using) to the sauce in the pan and bring to a fast boil for 2–3 minutes. Turn the heat down to a low simmer and stir in the cornflour paste, which will thicken the sauce, then once it is at a gravy-like consistency, taste and check the seasoning. Stir in the double cream, then add the chopped parsley and return the chicken breasts to the sauce. Stir and serve.

A BIT OF BAKING

Making your own baked goods needn't be over-complicated, and the simple fact is that the ingredients that go into 'home-made' foods can be controlled and adjusted to suit you and your family. I often play around with ingredients when I'm cooking, and I know from the number of questions I receive from followers that lower-sugar and gluten-free options are increasingly popular.

Let us start with a loaf of bread.

MY DAILY BREAD

I have said so many times that if there was only one food left that I could choose to eat, mine would be fresh bread. In fact, the end of the 'just-baked' loaf, still slightly warm, buttered, ready to be devoured. Yes please!

   I started making bread about 40 years ago after buying a bread machine. I loved it – it meant I could produce bread nearly as good as my grandmother's. I used to play around with various flour types, adding fruits and flavours, too, then after several years the bread machine gave up on me. It started to leave the paddle blade somewhere inside the loaf, or the loaf was misshapen, and then eventually the machine gave up completely and died. Instead of replacing it, I decided to make bread with my own hands. Artisan bread shops will bake beautiful speciality breads, but unfortunately where I live such an outlet is not available. And after all, I was familiar with the simple ingredients, I just had to understand the process that previously had been sorted out for me by the machine.

BASIC WHITE LOAF

MAKES 1 LOAF

Factory-produced, ultra-processed supermarket breads contain excess sugars and preservatives that are added to extend their shelf life, so if you fancy making your own, healthier loaf, this is the simplest of recipes.

500g strong plain
    white flour*, plus
    extra for dusting
7g active dried yeast
1 tsp sugar
320ml tepid water
5g salt
Spray of oil for the bowl
    (see home-made Spray
    Oil, page 216)

*Use any mix of flours –
going half and half with
white then adding
wholemeal, rye, spelt etc.
will give a light loaf with
extra flavour. For a seeded
loaf, add 1–2 tablespoons
of mixed seeds. If you find
yourself out of strong
flour, plain flour with a
little less protein (gluten)
will still produce a very
acceptable loaf.

You will need:
Digital weighing scales
Measuring jug
Measuring spoons
Tabletop food mixer
    fitted with a dough
    hook (optional)
Bench scraper
Spatula or wooden spoon
Large mixing bowl

TO MAKE THE DOUGH USING A MIXER:

Although packet yeast states it is unnecessary, I find my bread gets a better rise when I activate the yeast first. Place the yeast in the bottom of the mixing bowl of the mixer, add the sugar and about 100ml of the warm water. Swirl the sugar and yeast around in the bowl and wait a few minutes for the yeast to begin to froth.

You can skip this step, if you prefer, and you will still get a good loaf by simply adding the dried yeast and sugar to the bottom of the bowl, followed by the flour and then the salt. Add 300ml tepid water and start the machine.

If you prefer a loaf with no sugar at all, leave it out.

If you have decided to activate the yeast first, once frothy, add the flour, followed by the salt then 200ml more of the tepid water and mix on low speed until the ingredients are combined yet the dough looks shaggy. This may take several minutes.

The dough may be stuck around the hook in a solid lump at this point, and as a learner I used to think that was fine and ready to take from the machine and put to rise. However, the dough needs to feel soft and look smooth, and the more water the better for a light loaf.

So, if your dough is stuck, add half of the remaining water (10ml) and let the machine work at the dough for longer – if it still hugs the hook, add the remaining 10ml. The dough needs to look stretchy – as the gluten in the flour gets to work, it will cling to the bottom of the bowl rather than the hook. Increase the machine's speed and the dough will leave the sides and base of the bowl and will gather around the hook.

Recipe continued overleaf

Lightly dampened tea
    towel, reusable bowl
    cover or beeswax wrap
900g (2lb) loaf tin or
    baking sheet lined
    with reusable
    baking parchment
Cooling rack

TIP
If your kitchen is very
cold (like mine), a warm,
humid environment
perfect for proving bread
and yeasted products can
be achieved by boiling
a small amount of water
in a cup in the microwave
for 1–2 minutes. Remove
the cup and quickly
transfer the rising or
proving dough into
the warm steamy 'box'.

You will, with practice, learn to swiftly unlock the machine,
lift the lid, unscrew the dough hook and remove the dough
still attached in one go before gravity has the chance to drop
the dough from the hook back into the bowl. Use the bench
scraper to transfer the smooth, soft dough from the hook
onto a lightly floured surface.

Gently knead the ball of dough, which shouldn't feel too
sticky nor too dry, then drop it into a lightly oiled mixing
bowl, cover with a dampened tea towel, reusable bowl
cover, large plate or beeswax wrap and leave in a warm
place to rise until doubled in size. This can take between
30 and 60 minutes depending on the ambient room
temperature – bread dough loves a temperature of around
28°C (82°F) to rise in around 30 minutes, but it will take
longer at a lower temperature.

TO MAKE THE DOUGH BY HAND:

Add the yeast, sugar (if using), flour and salt to the bowl, then
pour in the warm water and use a spatula or wooden spoon
to mix the ingredients until well combined in a shaggy mix.

Turn out the very rough dough onto a clean work surface
and prepare yourself for a workout.

Kneading the dough may seem a messy affair to the newbie
bread baker but with practice you will develop your own
kneading rhythm that works for you. I push the dough forward
using the base of my right thumb (just above the wrist), then
pull it back towards me in one motion. I use the bench scraper
at the start to help release the sticky dough from the work
surface. Don't be tempted to add more flour – the more you
knead, the less sticky the dough becomes, and eventually
after around 10 minutes or so it will behave itself – you will
feel you are in charge and not the other way around.

Once the dough is smooth and soft, non-sticky and the work
surface and hands are clean, the dough can be transferred into
the oiled bowl, covered with the damp cloth, reusable bowl
cover or beeswax wrap and left to rise in a warm place until
doubled in size.

NEXT STEPS FOR MACHINE AND HAND-MADE DOUGH:

The dough will have risen up the sides of the bowl and now is the time for shaping. Lightly flour the work surface then use a spatula or wooden spoon to loosen the dough from the bowl and let it drop onto the surface. The dough should be warm, soft and full of air.

Use the bench scraper to gently fold the edges of the dough over and into the centre, then let the hands take over to gently but firmly 'knock back' the dough. This process will eliminate any large uneven air pockets that have formed as the yeast was doing its work.

To achieve a well-shaped, even loaf the dough now needs to be 'tightened'. To do this I form the dough into a ball and then twist it on itself, imagining this ball of dough was a huge bolt that I was trying to tighten using the heels of both hands. Screw this ball of dough clockwise until you feel the dough become rigid.

Flip the dough over, roll it into an oblong shape, then either place it into the bread tin, smooth-side uppermost, or leave it freeform on a baking sheet lined with reusable baking parchment. Leave to prove for 30–50 minutes. The timing depends on the ambient temperature: the warmer the environment, the faster the proving time. Dough in a tin can be popped straight into the preheated oven and the bread will rise up as it bakes. For a hand-shaped loaf, in order to give the expanding dough some direction you should slash the dough using a sharp serrated knife after the second prove and immediately before it goes into the oven. The easiest way is to dust flour over the surface then run the sharp knife swiftly and with purpose down the length of the dough, or make three shorter cuts. Don't hesitate – go for it. The dough may look worryingly flat after this attack, but put it straight into the hot oven and the dough will expand beautifully through the cut to produce a very attractive loaf.

Recipe continued overleaf

TIP
If you see your flour
crawling with small grey
insects, you probably have
weevils. Although flour
weevils are not poisonous
nor do they cause any
harm, if you detect them
in a bag of flour it can be
a shock. Historically, this
was one of the reasons
why flour was always
sifted before use. One tip
is to store flour in sealed
tins or airtight containers,
or you can add 2–3 fresh
bay leaves to the bag of
flour once opened. I leave
a bunch of fresh bay
hanging in the pantry,
too – partly so that I don't
always have to go outside
to pick it but also to keep
insects away.

Halfway through the second prove, preheat the oven to
220°C/200°C fan/425°F/gas 7. Slide the dough into the
oven and bake for 30 minutes until it is well risen, golden
brown and smelling delicious. If baked in a tin the bread
needs to be removed immediately after this time otherwise
the bottom of the loaf can go soggy because the steam
cannot escape. Remove the loaf from the tin/baking sheet
and transfer to a metal cooling rack to cool. I store bread
in a beeswax bread bag.

TIP
How do you know when the dough is sufficiently proved? The dough
will be doubled in size and when pushed lightly at the side with a
finger will bounce back and not leave an indentation. An overproved
dough will look flat and lifeless – a finger pushed against it will leave
a mark. Overproved dough when baked will not rise at all. If you see
that clearly the dough has overproved, it can be reshaped and left to
prove once more. The rise will not be as dramatic as it could have been
but better than wasting the dough. If you didn't realise the dough had
overproved, the bread is baked but did not rise – once cool, blitz it
to make Golden Breadcrumbs (see page 14)

TIP
Your home-baked loaf will become stale and hard after a couple
of days but it can be easily livened up. Spray with water then pop
into the microwave in 10-second bursts until it feels springy again.
Alternatively, for Aga owners whose oven is always on – spray with
water and pop into the top hot oven for 3–4 minutes.

A LIGHTER YET HEALTHY LOAF

MAKES 1 LOAF

When choosing bread, pay attention to the ingredients; for example, how much extra sugar is included and how much extra salt? Home-baked bread using just a few ingredients is better for us than highly processed factory-produced bread and if you are wanting to improve on my standard white bread recipe, here are a few options.

Wholemeal, spelt, rye and sprouted wholegrain flours are usually darker in colour and considered a healthier choice. Using whole wheat flours on their own can give a heavier bread – definitely more filling – though if you prefer a bread lighter in texture but still with extra health benefits over its 'all-white' partner, try mixing up the flours.

300g strong plain
    white flour, plus
    extra for dusting
200g wholemeal,
    spelt or rye flour
7g active dried yeast
1 tsp sugar
320ml tepid water
5g salt
2–3 tablespoons mixed
    seeds (optional)
Spray of oil for the bowl
    (see home-made Spray
    Oil, page 216)

You will need:
Digital weighing scales
Measuring jug
Measuring spoons
Tabletop food mixer
    fitted with a dough
    hook (optional)
Bench scraper
Spatula or wooden spoon
Large mixing bowl
Lightly dampened tea
    towel, reusable bowl
    cover or beeswax wrap
900g (2lb) loaf tin or baking
    sheet lined with reusable
    baking parchment
Cooling rack

Prepare the dough following the Basic White Loaf recipe on page 71, making your preferred flour choices and adding in the seeds at the kneading stage, if using.

For those living alone or who find that a whole loaf goes stale before it is eaten, or if there is limited time available for daily bread making, it is possible to get ahead and prep in advance. Why not make more than one batch of dough and freeze to prove and bake later?

I often make my standard bread recipe above then divide it between two x 450g (1lb) tins. One for now and one for when I am stuck for time – or for when I have come back from holiday and the last thing on my mind is bread-baking because I have all of the holiday laundry and the overgrown garden to catch up on!

All you need to do is shape the dough after the first rise, pop it into the tin, put the tin into a freezer bag and into the freezer. Alternatively, for a freeform loaf, shape the dough into a bloomer shape, pop onto a sheet of reusable baking parchment on a baking sheet and pop into the freezer. Once completely frozen and solid, remove from the sheet and baking parchment and into a freezer box or bag. Bread dough will freeze for up to 3 months.

TIP

I often take a tin of dough from the freezer, remove it from a freezer bag then place in the cold microwave with the door closed to defrost. I do this last thing at night and after 8 hours the dough has thawed, completed its rise and is ready to pop straight into the hot oven. I find this works better when the weather is cool – a hot spell of summer weather will mean the dough only takes 5 hours or so to thaw and will have overproved by the morning.

TIP

Save the unsalted cooking water from your potatoes and use in place of water for a lighter loaf.

TIP

You can replace the 1 teaspoon sugar with a drizzle of maple syrup or black treacle.

When ready to bake your loaf, take it from the freezer. You will notice that even in the time it took to freeze, your dough had already started to rise, then was halted in its tracks. Remove the tin and partly risen dough from the bag and transfer to your home-made proving oven (see page 72).

A 400–500g piece of frozen dough will take 5–8 hours to thaw and complete its second rise, depending on the ambient temperature. The dough will be ready to bake when it feels soft when pushed gently with a finger. At this point, pop it into a preheated oven for 25 minutes, by which time I have nearly unpacked and the washing machine is on.

GLUTEN-FREE BREAD

Following a significant number of questions and requests I decided to put time and effort into coming up with a decent gluten-free bread recipe. I had bought a gluten-free loaf in the past to taste the difference and although it was several years ago and the products I am sure are now much improved, the bread I tasted was dry, crumbly, tasteless and expensive.

When I browsed the supermarket shelves recently and 'homed in' on the section containing gluten-free ingredients and baked goods, I was shocked by the price – a very small loaf was three times the price of a supermarket wheat-flour equivalent! Then when I examined the packaging I was even more alarmed to discover a long list of ingredients and a sell-by date two months hence. The bread inside felt soft to the touch and had not one but two layers of plastic packaging – one plastic tray and a thick plastic bag to cover, making it a very expensive example of ultra-processed, factory-produced food. Not great for our health.

So if we are to try to avoid such foods along with their excess packaging I felt I had to do some work to help my gluten-free friends. Not to mention that baked goods with an eight-week shelf life are likely to be packed with ingredients that are not going to do our bodies a lot of good.

Can gluten-free bread be so expensive to make, I thought? Rather than research and try out other gluten-free recipes, I considered how best to develop a soft bread recipe of my own – that looks like a loaf of bread, tastes like bread, is not dry and crumbly and, just like a loaf made with wheat flour, will keep at least a few days.

I purchased a 1kg packet of gluten-free plain flour (enough to make 5 loaves) and set to work. I considered each ingredient carefully and only introduced it if it would add some benefit to the finished loaf. Although this recipe looks fairly simple, it took me some considerable time to perfect. Needless to say, I had to nip out for another bag of flour – it took seven attempts to get it right. 'Him indoors' seemed completely baffled, asking me what was wrong with our usual bread, and why was I making yet another loaf when the current one hadn't been used up? I had to get it just right …

A GLUTEN-FREE LOAF

MAKES 1 LOAF

This recipe has been so well received by my gluten-free and coeliac followers and has had great reviews, so give it a bash. I have included my Gluten-free Bread and Butter Pudding recipe on page 35 – it's easy to guess what I made with the leftovers!

1 tsp sugar or honey
  (feeds the yeast to
  help with the rise)
205ml warm water
  (for mixing)
1 tbsp potato starch
  (to give the yeast
  an additional boost)
5g active dried yeast
  (to rise the loaf)
180g gluten-free plain
  flour (no gluten)
25g ground almonds
  (for taste and colour)
5g salt (for taste and helps
  to keep the bread fresh)
½ tsp xanthan gum
  (to improve the crumb)
  or use 1 tsp psyllium
  husk powder
1 tbsp mayonnaise
  (to add moisture,
  richness, taste and
  help extend shelf life)

You will need:
Digital weighing scales
Measuring jug
Bowl
Whisk
450g (1lb) loaf tin,
  greased, or brushed
  with Gluten-Free
  Lining Paste (page 86)
Metal cooling rack

In a roomy mixing bowl add the sugar (or honey) and 100ml of the warm water and swirl around until the sugar is fully dissolved. Stir in the potato starch and yeast, then leave for 8–10 minutes until the yeast bubbles start to form. Use this time to weigh out the rest of the ingredients and lightly grease the tin or brush with lining paste.

Stir together the flour, almonds, salt and xanthan gum or psyllium husk powder and seeds, if using, and set aside.

Once the bowl containing the yeast has a bubbly froth on the surface then add the mix of dry ingredients and the mayonnaise and the rest of the water. Add the water little by little, stirring between each addition to avoid any lumps. Use a hand whisk to stir all of the ingredients together to a thick, smooth batter. Pour into the prepared tin and leave in the cold oven with just the light on. Put the timer on for 40 minutes.

After this time the batter should have risen to within 2 cm (¾ inch) of the top of the tin. If it hasn't quite got there yet, leave for another 5–10 minutes. If it gets there early, pop the oven on sooner. The speed the yeast reacts will depend on the ambient temperature – the colder the room, the slower the rise.

Once risen, leave the tin where it is and put the oven on to 180°C/160°C fan/350°F/gas 4 and set your timer for 45 minutes. My oven takes 15 minutes to achieve temperature and then I allow 30 minutes baking time. This dough doesn't benefit from being put into a preheated hot oven as the loaf rises too swiftly, and although the finished loaf at first looks appealing, once cut into there is a huge air pocket where some of the dough has risen but the rest has been left behind. A slow bake from cold allows the dough to rise slowly and evenly.

Recipe continued overleaf

Ten minutes before the end of the baking time (after 35 minutes), turn off the oven to save energy – leave the oven door closed and allow the bread to finish baking in the residual heat.

Take from the oven and remove from the tin while still warm, then leave to cool on a metal cooling rack.

Your gluten-free loaf will be well risen, golden brown, smelling like a delicious loaf of bread, cutting like a loaf of bread, soft, light and with a good crumb and – most importantly – will taste like bread should. No mysterious ingredients and cheaper than the supermarket alternatives.

LINING PASTE

An easy recipe to ensure your baked goods leave their tin smoothly.

Gluten-free (non-stick) lining paste can be made by whisking together 100g room-temperature butter, 100ml oil and 100g gluten-free plain flour to a thick paste. Keep in the fridge or freeze in small portions (maybe in a silicone ice-cube tray) if you don't bake often. Brush into tins and trays to ensure cakes, pastries, muffins, bundt cakes, etc. will easily release. It can also be made using wheat flour for a non-gluten-free version. If you need a dark lining paste for dark-coloured bakes, replace 20g of the flour with 20g cocoa powder.

MORE YEAST BAKING

ENGLISH MUFFINS

MAKES 9

For those wanting to make their own bread to avoid additional additives, but who don't have a bread machine and feel putting the oven on to bake just a loaf of bread is excessive and expensive, try making a batch of English muffins. There's no oven needed and the dough can be mixed and kneaded by hand then baked in a large frying pan on the hob. Delicious hot and buttered, used for sandwiches or toasted the next day.

110ml milk
½ tsp sugar
1 tsp active dried yeast
225g white bread flour
1 tsp salt
70ml water
Flour or semolina,
    for dusting
Oil or butter, for greasing

You will need:
Digital weighing scales
Measuring jug
Measuring spoons
Large microwave-safe
    mixing bowl
Wooden spoon or spatula
Plate, beeswax wrap,
    dampened tea towel
    or reusable bowl cover
Rolling pin
7.5cm (3 inch) plain
    round pastry cutter
Baking sheet, floured
Large heavy-based frying
    pan, very lightly greased
Timer
Cooling rack

Pour the milk into a microwave-safe bowl and microwave for 20 seconds until just warm. Add the sugar and dried yeast, then stir with the wooden spoon and set aside until it begins to froth (8–10 minutes). Add the flour and salt then stir, adding the water little by little until the dough is sticky.

Transfer the ball of dough to a clean work surface and begin to knead by hand. At first the dough will stick to your hands but gradually and eventually (after 10 minutes) it will have transformed from a shaggy mess to a smooth pillow of non-sticky dough. (See kneading notes on page 72.)

Pop the dough back into the mixing bowl, cover with a plate, beeswax wrap, dampened tea towel or reusable bowl cover and transfer to a warm place to rise until doubled in size.

When the dough has risen, transfer to a work surface dusted with flour or semolina and roll out to about 1.25cm (½ inch) thick and cut out nine 7.5cm (3 inch) rounds. You can reroll the trimmings as necessary. Transfer the muffins to a floured baking sheet and leave to prove for 25–30 minutes until risen to double their height.

Preheat the lightly greased frying pan over a medium heat then reduce the heat to low and add 4 muffins. Set the timer for 7 minutes then flip over and cook for another 7 minutes.

Transfer to a cooling rack and cook the next batch (I managed 5 in the pan this time).

Eat hot or toasted, spread with butter, or cold filled with a favourite filling.

CRUMPETS

MAKES 8

I love crumpets (often referred to as pikelets in the north of England) – the traditional English breakfast and teatime treat! These soft, spongy cakes, crispy on the outside, are served toasted and still warm with butter that readily oozes down into the little holes on their cratered surface. Crumpets originated in the seventeenth century but were brought up to date in the Victorian era when yeast and bicarbonate of soda were added. Enjoy them simply with butter, add jam, serve with a rasher of bacon or an egg – the possibilities are endless!

Home-made crumpets are lighter and more delicious than many of the rubbery shop-bought, factory-produced versions. Make them fun, too – use greased metal gingerbread-men or heart-shaped cookie cutters and the kids will enjoy them even more.

200ml warm water
5g sugar
4g active dried yeast
180g plain flour
4g salt
4g baking powder
30ml milk
Butter or oil for greasing,
  or use Lining Paste
  (page 86)

You will need:
Digital weighing scales
Measuring spoons
Microwave-safe bowl
Large mixing bowl
Spoon or fork
Sieve
Hand-held electric
  whisk or hand whisk
Flexible spatula
Plate, beeswax wrap,
  dampened tea towel
  or reusable bowl cover
7.5cm (3 inch) metal
  rings or metal cookie/
  pastry cutters

Start by warming the sugar in the water. I place my measured water in a microwave-safe bowl and pop it into the microwave for 40 seconds, or use warm water from a recently boiled kettle. Add the sugar and stir until it dissolves. The liquid needs to feel just warm, not hot. Add the yeast and stir well, then set aside for 10 minutes until you see that the yeast is activated and bubbles and froth are forming on the surface.

In a separate bowl, sift the plain flour, salt and baking powder then stir them together to combine. Add these dry ingredients to the bowl of frothed-up yeast, pour over the milk and stir to combine. Finish by mixing to a thick, smooth batter using the hand balloon whisk or electric hand whisk. Clean the sides of the bowl using the spatula to ensure there are no lumps stuck to the sides of the bowl. Cover with a plate, beeswax wrap, reusable bowl cover or a clean shower cap then leave in a warm place until doubled in size. See Tip on page 72.

After 50 minutes to an hour your batter will have formed bubbles on the surface, will be thicker and will have risen up the bowl. Take the heavy-based frying pan and rub the base with a little oil or butter – I use a butter paper. Grease the crumpet rings using butter/oil or brush with lining paste.

Recipe continued overleaf

Heavy-based frying pan
Non-contact food
thermometer (optional)
Large spoon or ladle for
transferring the batter
Small skewer or cocktail
stick (optional)
Fork, kitchen tweezers
or heatproof gloves
Metal spatula
Cooling rack

Place the pan and crumpet rings over a medium heat and allow to heat up gradually. If the fat starts to smoke, turn the heat or flame down slightly. If you have a non-contact food thermometer the temperature of the pan needs to be 180°C (350°F). If you don't have a non-contact food thermometer, I recommend a practice run first. Make just one crumpet, then you will understand exactly how hot your pan needs to be. A crumpet will need 10–12 minutes to cook all the way through. If the pan is too hot the base of your crumpet will burn before the top is cooked.

Using a ladle or large spoon, fill each ring or cutter about two-thirds full with the batter. Throughout the cooking time you will see the well-known little holes develop on the surface, starting at the edges. This is mesmerising and I find myself watching the theatrical show of bubbles slowly increasing in size then popping as the air escapes with glee from the surface of the crumpet. I like to get involved and enjoy giving the holes a helping hand using the end of a skewer or cocktail stick.

Once you are happy that all of the batter right through to the top of the crumpets is cooked and there is no wet or sticky batter on the surface, you can carefully remove the crumpet rings. They are very hot, so use a fork, protective gloves or kitchen tweezers to lift them off.

Flip the crumpets over using the metal spatula and brown the tops to a pale golden brown – this will take around 2 minutes.

Remove the crumpets from the pan, then leave to cool on a cooling rack to toast later. Your crumpets will keep in an airtight tin for a day or two or can be frozen at this stage then toasted on both sides once thawed. I have toasted them from frozen too!

If you are impatient and want to eat them immediately, cook them for longer, allowing the bases to brown to a deeper golden and the tops, too, then butter them while still hot.

DOUGHNUTS

MAKES 9

I adore fresh doughnuts – and the taste, texture, flavour and loveliness of a home-made doughnut cannot be matched by the ultra-processed supermarket equivalents.

A sweet treat should not be considered a sin when the home baker has carefully considered the ingredients that have gone into this delicious bake.

7g active dried yeast
1 large egg
75ml tepid milk
25g sugar
1 tsp Vanilla Extract
    (page 213)
20g soft room-
    temperature butter
230g white bread flour,
    plus extra for dusting
5g salt
30ml tepid water
Vegetable oil,
    for greasing and
    deep-frying
Approximately
    6 tbsp warmed jam
    (see page 241)
3–4 tbsp caster sugar,
    for dusting

You will need:
Tabletop mixer fitted
    with a dough hook
Jug
Digital weighing scales
Measuring jug
Measuring spoons
Large bowl
Plate or reusable
    shower cap
Baking sheet lined
    with reusable
    baking parchment
Deep-fat fryer
    or large pan

If you have a tabletop mixer fitted with a dough hook, the mixing is simple. Add the yeast to the bowl and then in a small jug mix together the egg, warm milk, sugar, vanilla extract and butter. Beat together with a fork then add to the yeast in the bowl. Add the flour then the salt and mix on a low speed until the dough is thick and shaggy looking. Add the water and continue to mix for about 5 minutes until the dough becomes smooth and stretchy. (The dough can also be mixed and kneaded by hand – follow tips on pages 71–2.)

Transfer the soft dough to a large bowl that has been sprayed with a little oil to prevent sticking, then cover with a plate or reusable shower cap. Leave in a warm place until doubled in size – this will probably take over an hour.

Take from the bowl and divide the dough into nine 50g pieces. Form these into balls and leave to prove on a baking sheet lined with baking parchment – for 1 hour or until doubled in size. I shut mine away in my home-made proving oven (see Tip on page 72).

Towards the end of the proving time, heat the oil in a large pan or deep-fat fryer to a temperature of 180°C (350°F) – the oil needs to be 7.5–10cm (3–4 inches) deep. Use the temperature probe to keep an eye on the temperature. Too hot and the doughnuts will burn before being cooked through, too cold and the doughnuts will be greasy and doughy.

Recipe continued overleaf

Temperature probe or
    non-contact food
    thermometer
Slotted spoon
Wooden spoon or spatula
Kitchen paper
Small saucepan or
    microwave-safe bowl
Piping bag fitted with
    long nozzle for jam
Skewer, thick cocktail
    stick or straw
Small bowl

TIP
To form the dough into
balls, take each 50g piece
of dough and fold it in on
itself (just as I did for the
large ball of dough when
making bread on page
73). Once the small piece
of dough is neatened to a
ball shape, turn it over so
that the rough turns are
on the underside, then
cup a hand over the top
of the ball and in a circular
motion form the dough
balls into neat, tight
shapes. The hand forms
a cage over the dough
and can tighten the
dough quickly and easily.

Fry in batches of 3 for 3–4 minutes on each side. The doughnuts
will bob and float as they cook and it is easy to see when the
undersides are golden brown and at this stage can easily be
flipped over using a wooden spoon or spatula. Fry until golden
brown on both sides then remove using a slotted spoon and
drain on kitchen paper.

The jam is easier to pipe into the doughnuts if it is heated
first, either in a small saucepan or for 20–30 seconds in the
microwave. Fill the piping bag with the warm jam then use
a skewer, thick cocktail stick or straw to make a hole in the
side of the doughnut. Fill each doughnut with jam while
still slightly warm, then roll in a small bowl containing
the caster sugar.

Best eaten within 2 days.

Enjoy . . .

HONEY BUNS

MAKES 12 BUNS OR 6 BUNS AND 1 900G (2LB) FRUIT LOAF

These light, semi-sweet bread buns filled with jam and cream are a delight – and I have to say they are one of my favourite bakes because they are light and lovely, not too sweet and can be dressed up to suit any occasion. I remember making these one summer day when friends were coming round and I served them as a dessert – making them colourful and fresh-looking using simply a squirt of cream and a display of summer berries.

They are absolutely delicious – I could eat one right now! To reduce the refined sugar content, I have sweetened the dough using honey rather than sugar. Although the recipe will make twelve buns, as they are best eaten on the day of baking I like to make just six and then bake a fruit loaf using the rest of the dough (page 99).

7g active dried yeast
500g white bread flour,
 plus extra for dusting
7g salt
250ml whole milk
50ml honey
1 large egg
1 tsp Vanilla Extract
 (page 213)
45g butter, melted
60ml tepid water

To fill 6 buns
300ml double cream
 whisked to soft peaks
 with 1 tsp icing sugar
3 tbsp jam (page 241)
 loosened with 1 tbsp
 water, or a selection
 of seasonal berries
 and fruits

You will need:
Digital weighing scales
Measuring jug
Measuring spoons
Tabletop mixer fitted
 with a dough hook
 (optional)

To make the dough using a tabletop mixer fitted with a dough hook, place the yeast into the mixing bowl, then the flour followed by the salt. In a large mixing jug, mix together the milk, honey, egg, vanilla and melted butter. Keep the warm water in a separate jug.

Pour the large jug of mixed liquids into the flour and mix on a low speed for about 10 minutes until the dough is smooth and stretchy. The dough needs to be fairly slack, not stuck into a huge ball. If your dough is dry and formed into a ball then you need to add more liquid. Add about half of the warm water from the other jug and continue to mix. Your dough is the right consistency when it leaves the sides of the bowl, sticks to the dough hook and can be lifted out of the machine in one piece. The dough should be shiny, smooth and elastic.

Transfer to a slightly floured work surface and knead by hand briefly to bring together to a smooth ball. If the dough is rough-looking it needs more mixing – pop it back into the mixer for 5 minutes and add more water. (Or mix the dough by hand, see notes on page 72.) When your dough looks as smooth as a pillow, start to shape it.

Recipe continued overleaf

Mixing jug
Separate jug for the water
Whisk
Mixing bowl
2 baking sheets lined
  with baking parchment
Metal cooling rack
Piping bag

For the buns, 70g of dough for each one is just right. Shape the weighed dough into balls (see tip on page 94) then transfer to a baking sheet lined with reusable baking parchment – allow 6 per baking sheet and space out well.

Leave the buns to rise – this can take what seems like a long time – about 1–1½ hours depending on the ambient temperature. They are ready to bake once doubled in size. (See Tip on speeding up proving by using the microwave on page 72.)

When ready to bake, preheat the oven to 210°C/190°C fan/ 425°F/gas 7.

Bake the buns for 16–18 minutes until well risen and golden brown.

Once baked, transfer the buns to a metal cooling rack to cool completely.

When cold, cut down the middle, open them out and pipe with fresh cream and a drizzle of raspberry jam, or create dessert showstoppers with a selection of seasonal fruits and fresh cream.

FRUIT LOAF

MAKES 2 900G (2LB) FRUIT LOAVES OR 4 450G (1LB) FRUIT LOAVES

I always make this fruit loaf at the same time as my Honey Buns on page 97, and it is delicious sliced and toasted. The quantities given could easily be halved if you only want to make one 900g (2lb) loaf, but they do freeze well if you wrap them in greaseproof paper.

7g active dried yeast
500g bread flour,
   plus extra for dusting
7g salt
250ml whole milk
50ml honey
1 large egg
1 tsp Vanilla Extract
   (page 213)
45g butter, melted
60ml tepid water
160g mixed dried
   fruit mixed with
   2 tsp mixed spice

You will need:
Digital weighing scales
Measuring jug
Measuring spoons
Tabletop mixer fitted
   with a dough hook
   (optional)
Mixing jug
Separate jug for the water
Rolling pin (optional)
Baking sheet lined
   with reusable
   baking parchment
2 x 900g (2lb) loaf tins
   or 4 x 450g (1lb) loaf
   tins if making the
   fruited loaf – greased
   or brushed with Lining
   Paste (page 86)
Metal cooling rack

Follow the method for making the dough for Honey Buns on pages 97–98.

Either use half the dough for 6 Honey Buns (page 97) and the remaining dough to make 1 x 900g (2lb) fruit loaf, remembering to halve the amount of dried fruit and spice, or use all of the dough for 2 x 900g (2lb) or 4 x 450g (1lb) loaves.

Simply spread the dough over a lightly floured work surface – a rolling pin can make this easier. Roll out to about 1.25cm (½ in) thick and scatter the spiced fruit over evenly. Roll up the dough using your hands, enclosing the fruit, then knead well to distribute evenly. Shape into two large or four small bloomer shapes (see tips on page 73) and transfer into the two large tins or four smaller loaf tins.

Leave the loaf or loaves to rise – this can take what seems like a long time – about 1–1½ hours depending on the ambient temperature. The fruit loaves are ready when the dough has crept up the sides of the tin. (See Tip on speeding up proving by using the microwave on page 72.)

When ready to bake, preheat the oven to 210°C/190°C fan/ 425°F/gas 7.

Bake the 450g (1lb) loaves for 20–25 minutes, and for a 900g (2lb) loaf for about 30 minutes.

Once baked, remove the fruit loaves from the tins while still hot, place on the cooling rack and leave to go completely cold.

The fruit loaves can be sliced and buttered or toasted. They will freeze well too.

SWEET TREATS

QUICK BANANA MUFFINS

MAKES 6

Don't discard that black-skinned banana that the kids refuse to eat – make these quick and delicious Quick Banana Muffins – they'll not turn their nose up at them. If you don't have the time to bake just now, peel the banana and pop it into a freezer bag or box to save either until you have more time or until you have a second banana and can make 12 muffins! This is a very quick mix and can easily be made and baked while the oven is on for something else.

1 ripe banana
50g brown sugar
60ml oil
1 large egg
110g self-raising flour
½ tsp ground mixed spice
   or ground nutmeg
40g chocolate chips
Icing sugar, for dusting

You will need:
Digital weighing scales
Mixing bowl
Fork
Hand-held electric whisk
Mixing spoon
Ice-cream scoop
6 deep muffin cases
6- or 12-hole muffin tin
Cooling rack

Preheat the oven to 180°C/160°C fan/350°F/gas 4.

Mash the banana in a bowl with a fork, add the sugar, oil and egg and whisk with the hand-held electric whisk. Add the flour and spice and stir to combine. Finally, fold in the chocolate chips.

Use a large spoon or ice-cream scoop to divide the batter evenly among 6 deep muffin cases set into a 6- or 12-hole tin. Bake for 20–25 minutes until risen and firm to the touch.

Transfer to a cooling rack to cool completely, then serve dusted with icing sugar.

TIP
Out of brown sugar? Make your own! Place 200g white granulated sugar into a roomy microwave-safe mixing bowl, drizzle over 20–25g black treacle then pop into the microwave for 10–15 seconds (or a warm oven if you don't have a microwave). Take from the microwave and rub together as though rubbing fat into flour. The softened treacle and warm sugar will come together beautifully and will look and taste just the same as the more expensive shop-bought version. Store in a glass jar with a screw-top lid and it will remain free flowing.

JAMAICAN-STYLE GINGER CAKE

MAKES 2 450G (1LB) CAKES OR 1 900G (2LB) CAKE

This is one of those cakes I used to pull from the supermarket shelf and it is a real favourite, having been around for as long as I can remember.

I would eat it on its own or slice it and then give it a quick blast in the microwave to heat it up, and I used to serve it with custard when the children were small.

This recipe is dark, moist and utterly delicious. Make just one cake if you wish, but I tend to think that if the oven is going on anyway, why not make two? One for now and one for a friend or the freezer. Or make one large cake in a 900g (2lb) loaf tin. This cake improves and becomes more moist after a day or two in an airtight tin and will keep for a week to ten days.

200g self-raising flour
    or gluten-free
    self-raising flour
1 tsp baking powder
1 tbsp ground ginger
1 tsp ground cinnamon
1 tsp mixed spice
60g black treacle
80g golden syrup
100g dark brown sugar
100g butter
180ml whole milk
2 large eggs

You will need:
Digital weighing scales
Measuring jug
Measuring spoons
2 x 450g (1lb) loaf tins
    or 1 x 900g (2lb) loaf
    tin, well greased or
    brushed with Dark
    Lining Paste (page 86)
Pastry brush
Mixing bowl
Sieve
Medium saucepan
Wooden spoon
Spoon
Airtight storage tin

Preheat the oven to 190°C/170°C fan/375°F/gas 5. Start by brushing the loaf tin(s) with dark lining paste.

In a large roomy mixing bowl, sift together the flour, baking powder and spices. In a medium saucepan and over a low heat, melt together the treacle, syrup, sugar and butter and stir until the butter melts, the sugar dissolves and the mixture is well combined. Do not allow to boil.

Make a well in the centre of the flour in the bowl using a spoon and pour over the melted ingredients. Beat the measured amount of milk with the two eggs in a jug then add this a little at a time to the thick batter.

Pour the thin mixture into the tin or tins and bake in the oven for 40 minutes, until risen and firm to the touch. The 900g (2lb) tin will take an hour to bake.

Remove from the oven and leave the cake or cakes to cool in the tin or tins. Once cool, remove from the baking tin and transfer to an airtight tin, where it will improve and become more sticky and gooey after a day of storage. This cake freezes very well too.

TIP

If you have a jar of my dried Citrus Crumb (page 226), try adding 2 tbsp of it to the dry ingredients and stir through. A sprinkle can also be dusted over the finished cake. To make it adhere, first brush with a simple sugar syrup – 2–3 tsp sugar dissolved in 2 tsp water in a small saucepan or 10–20 seconds in the microwave then brushed sparingly over the warm cake.

SPICED BREAD

MAKES 1 900G (2LB) LOAF

This easy recipe ticks many boxes – it's fat-free and egg-free, and it can be easily adapted to be gluten-free, or low in refined sugar, or you can omit the ground almonds and extract for a nut-free version. And if you like you can switch maple syrup for honey for a vegan-friendly cake. It's also budget friendly, as it will bake happily in the oven alongside another dish.

This is such a delicious bake that improves in flavour after a day or two if kept in an airtight tin wrapped in foil or greaseproof paper, and is delicious on its own or spread with a little butter. Remember to keep 4 thin slices back to use to thicken and flavour the Beef in Beer casserole recipe on page 64.

280g honey or
   maple syrup
50g dark brown sugar
1 tsp almond extract
40ml rum, brandy,
   or black tea for an
   alcohol-free cake
160g mixed dried fruits
100ml boiling water
200g flour (gluten-free,
   plain, rye, wholemeal
   – I use malted grain
   bread flour)
70g ground almonds
   (or use the same
   amount of flour
   for a nut-free cake)
2½ tsp ground
   mixed spice
½ tsp Chinese 5 spice
Pinch of salt
2 tsp baking powder

You will need:
900g (2lb) loaf tin,
   well greased or
   brushed with dark
   Lining Paste (page 86)
2 mixing bowls
Stick blender
Hand-held electric whisk
Digital weighting scales

Weigh the honey or maple syrup into one of the mixing bowls along with the brown sugar, almond extract, rum, brandy or tea, mixed dried fruits and boiling water. Blitz with a stick blender to a thick batter then set aside.

In a separate bowl, weigh the flour, almonds, spices, salt and baking powder and stir well.

Use the hand-held electric whisk to quickly mix the dry ingredients into the thick batter. Transfer to the prepared tin and bake at 170°C/150°C fan/350°F/gas 4 for 1 hour.

Remove from the oven, leave the cake to cool in the tin then turn out, wrap in foil and pop into an airtight tin for a day or two. The cake will then mature in flavour, be easier to slice and taste delicious.

THE ULTIMATE (THREE-LAYER) CHOCOLATE CAKE

MAKES 1 CAKE

A chocolate cake, for me, has to be dark in colour, moist yet light in texture, and most of all it must taste of chocolate. It took me some time to perfect this sponge. For the buttercream filling I have chosen to create a velvety smooth, dark chocolate buttercream, which is so easy to make, not too sweet and is very well behaved, being perfect for smoothing and piping. You will probably not want to make any other chocolate buttercream after trying this.

For the cakes:
110g dark chocolate, broken into chunks
65g cocoa powder
2 tsp Vanilla Extract (page 213)
225ml whole milk
270g soft spreadable butter, room-temperature butter or margarine
240g caster sugar
2 tbsp black treacle or golden syrup
4 large eggs
270g self-raising flour

For the buttercream:
130g dark chocolate, broken into chunks
250g room-temperature salted butter (not spreadable butter or margarine)
20g cocoa powder
1 tsp Vanilla Extract (page 213)
397g tin condensed milk

You will need:
3 7.5 x 18cm (3 x 7 inch) sandwich cake tins, greased and lined with baking paper, sides brushed with Dark Lining Paste (page 86)

Preheat the oven to 190°C/170°C fan/375°F/gas 5. Grease and line the cake tin bases with baking paper and brush the sides with dark lining paste.

To make the cakes, put the chocolate chunks into a small bowl set over a pan of recently boiled water, off the heat, and leave to melt gently, stirring occasionally. Once melted, take the bowl off the pan and set aside.

In a separate bowl, combine the cocoa powder and vanilla extract, then add the measured milk, stirring it in little by little until you have a smooth, thin chocolate paste. Set aside.

In a large mixing bowl, cream the butter and sugar together with the hand-held electric whisk until light and fluffy then add the black treacle or golden syrup and whisk well to combine. Add the eggs one at a time, whisking well between each addition to avoid a curdle. Sift the flour and add to the batter, folding it in slowly and thoroughly by hand with a metal spoon, not the whisk.

Once you have a smooth yet thick batter, add the cocoa/milk paste and stir well to make sure there are no flecks of light-coloured batter remaining, then finally stir in the melted and cooled chocolate.

Recipe continued overleaf

Digital weighing scales
Measurign jug
Measuring spoons
2 small bowls
Saucepan
2 large mixing bowls
Hand-held electric whisk
Sieve
Metal spoon
Cooling racks
Serrated knife
Spirit level (optional)
Bench scraper
Reusable piping bag
    and nozzles

TIP
If your batter or
buttercream should split
and curdle, don't discard
it because it can be fixed.
The cake batter can be
rectified by adding
1 tbsp flour to the mix
and whisking well.
Curdled buttercreams
can look unappealing
and spoilt but all you
need to do is spoon out
1–2 tbsp into a small
mug or microwave-proof
bowl and pop into the
microwave for 10 seconds
or until you see the curdled
cream become a thick
liquid. With the whisks
going, pour the warm
liquid into the buttercream
and before your eyes the
buttercream will return
to its former glory.

Divide evenly between the three tins using weighing scales to ensure even-sized finished sponge layers. Transfer to the oven and bake for 25–30 minutes until the cakes are evenly risen and firm to the touch. The cakes will probably rise with a slight dome, but as they cool in the tins they will flatten out and start to leave the sides of the tin. Leave to cool slightly in the tins, then when completely cool, take out of the tins, peel away the base paper and transfer to cooling racks.

To make the buttercream, put the broken chocolate into a heatproof bowl set over a pan of recently boiled water and leave to melt gently, or melt in the microwave in 30-second bursts, stirring well in between. Once melted, remove the bowl from the pan.

In a roomy mixing bowl place the soft butter, cocoa powder and vanilla extract, and with the whisk on its lowest speed blend them together so that you have a very thick, dark-coloured creamed mix. Once the cocoa powder has blended in, increase the whisk speed and whisk until fluffy.

Add the condensed milk 2 tablespoons at a time, whisking well between each addition until the whole tin has been added. Whisk until the cream is looking light, smooth and silky. Whisk in the cooled melted chocolate and the buttercream is ready to use.

To assemble the cakes, if the sponges have domed slightly then slice off the tops with a serrated knife before stacking and filling each layer with buttercream. As I stack the cakes I use a small spirit level to ensure the cake is straight and flat. Then add a crumb coat of buttercream, smooth off and chill in the fridge for at least an hour so that the cake and filling can firm up.

Take from the fridge and use the rest of the buttercream to apply a top coat, then smooth the icing with a bench scraper and decorate.

COURGETTE CUPCAKES

MAKES 9–10 CUPCAKES OR 1 CAKE

When courgettes are in season you will find them cheaply in the shops, and if you grow them yourself you will be looking for ways to keep up with their fast-growing zest for life.

Overgrown courgettes (the ones you come back to following a holiday) can be used to make my Courgette Cannelloni on page 29, but this recipe makes excellent use of the small beautiful ones. Use yellow courgettes for a lemon version and the green ones for lime.

I have friends who told me they are not fans of courgettes and would never want to buy, grow or eat them – then they tasted these cupcakes!

250g yellow or green courgettes (young veg without seeds)
Finely grated zest of 1 large lemon (or 2 limes if using green veg)
2 large or 3 medium eggs
190g caster sugar
160ml oil
290g self-raising flour

For the icing
Juice of the lemon/limes
icing sugar
extra zest or sprinkles, to decorate

You will need:
12-hole cupcake tin and paper cases or 20cm (8 inch) square, loose-bottomed cake tin well greased or brushed with Lining Paste (page 86)
2 large mixing bowls
Coarse grater
Lemon zester
Digital weighing scales
Hand-held electric whisk
Sieve
Large metal spoon
Cooling rack
Small bowl

Preheat the oven to 190°C/170°C fan/375°F/gas 5. Fill the holes of the cupcake tin with paper cases, if making cupcakes.

Start by grating the courgettes into a large mixing bowl using a coarse grater. Add the lemon or lime zest, stir, then set aside.

In a second mixing bowl, whisk together the eggs and sugar for about 5 minutes with the hand-held electric whisk, until the mixture is pale and increased in volume and the whisks leave a trail on the surface of the mix when lifted. Add the oil and whisk again, then sift over the flour and fold in with a large metal spoon. Take your time – no bashing of that light batter – stir gently until all of the flour is incorporated.

When everything is well combined, add the bowl of grated courgettes, mix well, and transfer to the prepared tin or divide between 9–10 paper cases. Bake cupcakes for 25–30 minutes or cake for 35–40 minutes until golden, risen and firm to the touch. Remove from the tin and transfer to a cooling rack.

While the cake cools, mix a water icing. Simply add the sifted icing sugar to the lemon or lime juice and stir until the mix has the consistency of thick pouring cream. Pour this over the cooled cake and spread to the edges, or drizzle over cupcakes. Scatter over some lemon zest or sprinkles.

TIPS

A foil collar wrapped around the outside of the cake tin will diffuse the heat while baking to ensure an even bake and a flat top. Can be reused.

To achieve slices with clean, neat edges, pop the finished cake into the freezer for about 20 minutes to firm up before slicing.

BAKED LIME, CHOCOLATE & COCONUT CHEESECAKE

SERVES 12–16

I decided to include this recipe because I realise this three-flavour combo hasn't been used across any other recipe in the book, but more importantly because I remember the huge disappointment the first time I ever tried to bake a cheesecake. You know how it is – you have invested in the ingredients, done exactly what the recipe says, yet the result is not great and it puts you off ever having a go at that particular bake, let alone recipe, ever again. With that in mind, I thought I didn't want other bakers to make the same mistakes as me, so I considered a few extra tips may be useful.

I recall my 'baked cheesecake disaster' – even though I followed the recipe to the letter, the end result was rubbery, had a crack across the middle, was brown at the sides and pretty tasteless with a thick, hard base. A lot of it ended up in the bin. For this reason I avoided baked cheesecakes for years afterwards.

Some time later, armed with more knowledge and experience, I managed this very delicious baked cheesecake. Although it can be baked in a round tin, when made in a square tin, sliced into fingers and easily decorated, it can look amazingly 'top end'.

Lime, chocolate and coconut are one of my favourite flavour combinations and they certainly come together beautifully in this dessert. This can also be easily adapted to be gluten-free by switching the chocolate digestive biscuits to gluten-free ones.

For the base:
120g plain chocolate
   digestive biscuits
70g butter
¼ tsp Chinese 5 spice
   (optional)

For the filling
500g full-fat cream
   cheese at room
   temperature
100g caster sugar
1 tbsp cornflour
Finely grated zest
   and juice of 3 limes
   (keep a little zest
   back for decoration)
400g tin of
   condensed milk
3 large eggs, beaten

Begin by lining the base and sides of the cake tin with aluminium foil then set aside. Preheat the oven to 180°C/160°C fan/350°F/gas 4.

Break the chocolate biscuits into fine crumbs. This can be done quickly in a food processor or alternatively use a strong freezer bag and a rolling pin. Break the biscuits into large pieces by hand, pop them into the bag, seal it, then roll the biscuits and the bag with the rolling pin on a work surface. Regularly lift up the bag to jiggle the biscuits around then re-roll until all lumps are gone.

Recipe continued overleaf

For the topping:
400ml tin of full-fat
    coconut milk, chilled
100ml double cream
1 tsp icing sugar
Lime zest and
    chocolate sprinkles,
    flakes or cocoa
    powder, to decorate

You will need:
23cm (9 inch) loose-
    bottomed round cake
    tin or 20cm (8 inch)
    square loose-bottomed
    cake tin lined with foil
Food processor or strong
    freezer bag (optional)
Rolling pin
Digital weighing scales
Measuring jug
Measuring spoons
Zester
Small saucepan
Large mixing bowl
Spatula or wooden spoon
Small angled palette knife
Hand-held electric whisk
Aluminium foil
Large, deep roasting tin
    (larger than the size
    of the tins above)
Wire cooling rack
Large plate
Piping bag and nozzle
Fine grater for lime zest

In a small saucepan, melt the butter for the base then add the spice (if using) and biscuit crumbs. Stir well then transfer into the base of the cake tin. The base of this cheesecake needs to be very thin and delicate, so take your time spreading out the crumbs. It may seem that there aren't enough to go around, but I found that an old teaspoon bent at right angles works well at getting into the corners of a square tin. A small angled palette knife is helpful too.

Once the crumbs are in an even compacted and smooth layer, bake for just 3 minutes then remove from the oven and allow to cool completely. Turn the oven down to 170°C/150°C fan/325°F/gas 3.

In a roomy mixing bowl place the cream cheese and sugar and whisk together until smooth. Add the cornflour, lime zest and juice, condensed milk and beaten eggs together, then whisk everything together well using the hand-held electric whisk.

Take a large sheet of foil and wrap this around the 'outside' of the prepared tin containing the biscuit base. Wrap in a second layer of foil to make it watertight, then place this into the large roasting tin. Baking the cheesecake in a bain-marie (water bath) is the secret to a successful baked cheesecake. The extra effort here will prevent burning to the outside of the cheesecake and cracking in the centre.

Once the prepared tin is in place in the roasting tin then the filling can be added. Pour the filling over the biscuit base and smooth out. Take a kettle of boiling water and pour this into the roasting tin so that it comes about 5cm (2 inches) up the sides of the foil-covered cheesecake tin.

Place carefully into the oven and bake for just 30 minutes. Then turn off the oven, open the door slightly and leave the cheesecake in the oven for 1 hour. Remove from the oven – the cheesecake will have a wobble in the centre and this is perfect. Take the cheesecake from the water bath and cool on a wire rack. When completely cold, cover with a plate and chill overnight.

To line a tin with foil quickly and easily and without putting your fingers through, turn the tin upside down and mould the foil around the outside of the tin, paying particular attention to the corners when lining a square tin. Fold the corners neatly. When lining a round tin simply use your hands to ensure the foil hugs the shape of the tin. Lift the pre-moulded piece of foil and gently slide to the inside of the tin, easing into the corners.

The next day, remove the chilled cheesecake from the tin, remove the loose base, then carefully peel away the foil and transfer the cheesecake to a presentation plate using a cake slice or use the already removed loose bottom of the tin to double up as a cake slice.

Whisk the solids from the chilled coconut milk (pour off the liquid first), with the double cream and icing sugar. Transfer this mixture to a piping bag. Try scoring the surface of the cheesecake to mark out the portions then pipe between the lines. It makes cutting and serving the slices so much easier and neater. Complete the deliciousness with a scattering of lime zest and chocolate sprinkles, flakes or a light dusting of cocoa powder.

BAKED LEMON CHEESECAKE

For a lemon cheesecake, use plain digestive biscuits (or gluten-free digestive biscuits) for the base, swap the limes for 2 large lemons, and make the topping using 300ml double cream whisked with 1 teaspoon vanilla extract and 2 tablespoons icing sugar. Decorate with fresh lemon zest.

CHOCOLATE BROWNIES

MAKES 16 SQUARES OR 8–10 SLICES

Chocolate brownies are a popular bake and one seen so often among the ultra-processed family of ready-made bakes on the supermarket shelves, with an alarming way-into-the-future use-by date thrown in for good measure! In addition, you may also see packs of expensive dried mixes that say 'simply add eggs and butter', often with a single-use plastic baking tray, too.

As we are staying away from ultra-processed convenience foods, excess packaging and single-use plastic items, I decided to include my recipe, which is easy to make and I have to say as well as being a welcome baked treat with a cup of tea or coffee, a warm brownie served with a warm (boozy) Espresso Sauce (see page 212) and a blob of Easy Vanilla Ice Cream (see page 214) makes for the perfect adult dessert!

Another bonus is that all the ingredients are mixed together in a saucepan, so this recipe is great if you hate washing up.

200g butter or margarine
200g brown sugar
1 tsp Vanilla Extract
  (page 213)
150g dark chocolate,
  broken into chunks
  (I use 70% cocoa
  solids for flavour)
90g plain flour
60g cocoa powder
2 large eggs

You will need:
Digital weighing scales
Measuring spoons
Large saucepan
Wooden spoon or spatula
Sieve
Fork
20cm (8 inch) square
  loose-bottomed
  cake tin, lined with
  greaseproof paper
Angled palette knife

Preheat the oven 190°C/170°C fan/375°F/gas 5.

In a large saucepan add the butter, sugar and vanilla. Stir over a gentle heat until the butter melts and the sugar dissolves, then take off the heat. Add the chocolate chunks to the pan, stir, then set aside until the chocolate slowly melts into the warm mixture. Once the chocolate has melted and the mix is smooth and silky, sift over the flour and cocoa. Stir into the mix then add the two eggs. Beat well to combine.

Transfer the mixture to the prepared tin and level it with the back of a spoon or an angled palette knife. Bake for 20–25 minutes then place on a cooling rack, still in the tin, and allow to cool completely.

Once cold, remove from the tin, remove the paper then cut into 16 neat 5cm (2 inch) squares or 8–10 slices. These brownies will keep in an airtight tin for at least a week.

TIP
To line your tin, stand it on a square of greaseproof paper and use a pencil to draw around. Turn the paper over so that the pencil lines will not come into contact with the cake. Fold inwards along each of the lines, then snip each of the four corners from the edge up to the point where each crease crosses. Pop into the tin for a perfect fit – the paper tabs will tuck perfectly behind the paper-lined side.

FAMILY
FAVOURITES

Delicious, nutritious food that will feed a few or a crowd, depending on
the size of your family and who else might have dropped in at teatime.
These recipes are versatile and batch-friendly too so you can get ahead
at the weekend ready for the midweek rush.

FISH FINGERS

MAKES 10–12 FISH FINGERS DEPENDING ON SIZE OF FILLETS

A popular favourite with both children and adults, fish fingers are a quick and convenient meal choice for many families, although when I flipped over the mass-produced supermarket pack I found I was only getting 64 per cent fish in my fingers – some brands even as low as 58 per cent! When home-made your fish fingers will be in the region of 90% fish! I did a test weight of my piece of fish – 20g for a small finger, then egged and crumbed it weighed 23g. Making your own is quick and easy and can actually work out cheaper depending on your choice of fish – cod is used in some fish fingers, as is pollock, but I like to use hake here. Fish fingers can be shallow-fried, oven-baked or air-fried.

250g skinless,
    boneless white fish
1 large egg, beaten
3–4 tbsp Golden
    Breadcrumbs (page 14)
Spray of oil (make your
    own, page 216)

You will need:
Kitchen paper
Sharp knife
Chopping board
2 bowls or shallow dishes
Plate or board
Air fryer, baking sheet
    or frying pan

Dry the fish on kitchen paper then cut into finger-sized pieces lengthways – do not cut across the fillet because it will break as it cooks. Cutting lengthways may result in some fingers being a bit misshapen and skinny in places, but that's the beauty of home-made.

Add the egg to a bowl then add the breadcrumbs to another bowl. Dip the fish pieces first into the beaten egg then roll in the breadcrumbs. When covered all over, transfer to a plate or board. I use just one hand for this, keeping one hand clean just in case I need to reach for more breadcrumbs. Once the fish fingers are well coated, chill or pop into the freezer for 10 minutes or so. I find fish fingers easier to handle when chilled firm or partly frozen.

When ready to cook, heat a spray of oil in a frying pan and fry the fish fingers for 2–3 minutes on each side until golden and the fish is cooked through. If you are air-frying, preheat the air fryer for 5 minutes then spray the fish fingers with a little oil on both sides and cook for 6–8 minutes until golden and cooked through. To oven-bake, preheat the oven to 200°C/180°C fan/400°F/gas 6 with a baking sheet inside, and once hot add the fish fingers, spray with oil and bake for 12–15 minutes, turning halfway through.

12-HOUR SLOW-COOKED RAGU

SERVES 8-10

There are so many recipes for this classic Italian sauce, each chef adding this or that to make it their own. My recipe is simple, economical and has few ingredients, but most of all it has a rich, deep flavour that's achieved from the long, slow cooking.

I no longer bother to fry the minced meat first before cooking – it makes absolutely no difference to the finished flavour, in my opinion, and is just a needless use of excess valuable energy (and cooking smells). So my recipe is easy and quick to prepare – and then you can forget about it.

Traditionally served with tagliatelle (see Fresh Pasta on page 219), ragu Bolognese is also often served with spaghetti or any pasta of choice and makes a great base for lasagne or for the Courgette Cannelloni on page 29. The recipe below will serve 8–10 people, depending on portion size, though if I am going to the effort of making it I make double this amount then freeze it in portions so that we have a quick meal to come home to when I have been out for the day, or gardening, shopping, writing, working or feeling just too lazy to cook. I usually serve 8 people from this recipe – 4 for a lasagne and 4 for Bolognese served with pasta.

2 tbsp oil (olive oil can be expensive, so use your oil of choice)
2 rashers of streaky bacon, chopped, or bacon lardons, smoked or unsmoked
1 large onion or 2 small onions, finely chopped
1 heaped tsp dried mixed herbs
1 tsp ground nutmeg
250g minced pork
250g minced beef
2 carrots, cut into 5mm (¼ inch) dice
4–5 garlic cloves, cut into 5mm (¼ inch) dice
2 celery sticks, cut into 5mm (¼ inch) dice
80ml red wine
250ml good chicken stock (see Stock Cubes on page 206)

Heat the oil in the casserole dish, frying pan or bowl of a multi-cooker and add the bacon, onions, dried herbs and nutmeg, then give everything a stir and let the ingredients fry gently over a low heat for about 10 minutes.

Once the onions are softened, turn up the heat and add the minced pork and beef, using the wooden spoon to break it up, move it around the pan and gently brown. Don't spend too long on this – 5 minutes or so – then add the diced veggies, wine, stock, passata or tomatoes, salt and pepper and tomato puree.

Give everything a thorough stir, put the lid on and cook in the slow cooker on high for 11 hours (see Note), in the bottom (simmering) oven of the Aga for 12 hours or the oven at 110°C/90°C fan/225°F/gas ¼ for 12 hours.

After the cooking time is up, check the seasoning, adjusting as necessary. I actually prefer to allow this ragu to go completely cold and reheat it the next day as I think the flavours improve, but you will not be disappointed if you eat it straight away.

Recipe continued overleaf

800g chopped tomatoes
(2 tins), Italian passata,
or my Passata (page 42)
1 tsp each of salt
and pepper
2 tbsp tomato puree

You will need:
Chopping board
and knife
Digital weighing scales
Large ovenproof casserole
dish with a well-fitting
lid, 4L multi or slow
cooker that allows you
to fry too. Otherwise
start the onions in a
frying pan then transfer
to the slow cooker.
Wooden spoon

Note: If your slow cooker doesn't permit frying then fry
the onions and bacon in a frying pan in the oil then transfer
to the slow cooker and add everything else.

SPAGHETTI BOLOGNESE

Cook your spaghetti (or dried pasta of choice) according to
the packet instructions, allowing approximately 60–90g dried
pasta per person (or buy or make your own fresh – 100g to
120g per serving – see page 219).

Cook home-made pasta in well-salted boiling water for
2–5 minutes then drain briefly, retaining a little water, then
add about a dessertspoon of oil. Transfer to a warm serving
plate before topping off with around 3 large tablespoons of
hot ragu then add a grating of Parmesan cheese.

HOW TO JOINT A CHICKEN:

Take the whole chicken and place it on a board in front of you. First, remove the legs. To do this, pull a leg away from the body and score the skin between the leg and body. Do this for both legs. Take a leg in each hand and pull downwards and you will feel the bone unhook from the main carcass. Take the point of a knife and cut through the sinew and remove the legs. Set aside.

To remove the breasts, take the point of the knife and score along the breast bone – keep going until the breast can be carefully removed. Continue to slide the knife down using the rib cage as a guide, holding the knife in one hand and the chicken breast in the other. Remove the two chicken breasts and set aside. There will be a fillet attached to each of the breasts and these can be left on.

If the chicken is quite small I leave the wings on the bird.

The first time you do this you may be left with quite a lot of meat on the carcass, but don't worry – it will be used for the Coq au Leekie Bean Stew on page 138 or Chicken Stock on page 140.

From the two chickens I have four legs, four breasts and two carcasses. Here are my favourite recipes for using them.

The Four Legs
CIDER CHICKEN WITH MUSHROOMS & TARRAGON

SERVES 4

I have a hardy Russian tarragon plant that shows its leaves every springtime and will continue until the first frosts. It is stronger in flavour than French tarragon and works well in this chicken dish, which is made in about an hour in the oven, on the hob or in a multi-cooker.

2 tbsp oil of choice
4 chicken legs, skin on
8 shallots, peeled but
    left whole
8 garlic cloves, peeled
    and left whole
150g chestnut
    mushrooms, cut in half
500ml cider or 250ml
    apple juice and
    250ml water
1 tbsp vinegar
1 tbsp cornflour mixed
    to a thin paste with
    2–3 tbsp cold water
1 tbsp crème fraîche,
    double cream or
    single cream
1 bunch of fresh tarragon
    or 2 tbsp dried
Salt and pepper

You will need:
Large frying pan with
    a lid or casserole
    dish with lid
Measuring jug
Measuring spoons
Chopping board
Knife
Plate

Start by heating the oil in a large frying pan or casserole dish on the hob or in the bowl of a multi-cooker. Season the chicken portions on both sides with salt and pepper then pop them skin-side down into the hot fat. Leave to fry for 5–10 minutes or until the skin is a deep golden brown; don't turn them over. Turn the heat down then remove from the pan onto a plate. Add the shallots and garlic cloves to the hot frying pan and toss these around until they are golden brown. Using a slotted spoon, remove from the pan and onto the plate with the chicken.

Brown the mushrooms until they are lightly coloured too and transfer to the plate with the chicken. With the heat on its lowest setting, pour into the pan the cider (or apple juice and water) and vinegar – it will fizz but will deglaze the pan beautifully. Stir, then add the cornflour paste to thicken the sauce. Stir it thoroughly into the cider and bring to a gentle simmer. When the sauce is thickened stir through the crème fraîche or cream.

Add the chicken, mushrooms, garlic and shallots back into the pan. Strip the leaves from the tarragon stalks and sprinkle about two-thirds amongst the chicken and sauce. Season again with salt and pepper then either simmer very gently on the hob, partly covered, for 1 hour or transfer to the oven set at 200°C/180°C fan/400°F/gas 6 for the same length of time. Alternatively, transfer to a slow cooker for 3–4 hours or the multi-cooker for 1 hour at 190°C. The sauce should be thick and flavoursome – if it is too thin, cook without a lid for 10 minutes so until the sauce thickens. Serve with potatoes and a green vegetable.

The Four Legs

MEDITERRANEAN CHICKEN WITH SWEET PEPPERS

SERVES 4

If you grow your own tomatoes and peppers this recipe is simply perfect. I enjoy this especially during the summer months, though I use frozen peppers and stored passata during the winter months for a taste of summer. This can be made in the slow cooker, oven, hob or pressure cooker.

Oil, for frying
4 chicken legs, skin on
1 small courgette
    (or 2 tbsp capers from
    a jar), cut into small dice
3–4 garlic cloves, chopped
2 red peppers, deseeded
    and sliced, or 200g
    frozen pepper pieces
2 tbsp black olives
    from a jar
Handful of fresh
    basil leaves, plus
    extra to garnish,
    or 1–2 tbsp pesto
1 tbsp dried mixed herbs
½ fresh mild red chilli,
    finely chopped or pinch
    of dried chilli flakes
1 tsp paprika
2 x 400g tins of
    chopped tomatoes
    or 800g passata

You will need:
Large ovenproof frying
    pan with a lid or
    casserole dish with a lid
Chopping board
    and knife
Measuring spoons
Wooden spoon
Large plate

Heat the oil in the ovenproof frying pan or casserole dish or the bowl of a multi-cooker and fry the chicken legs skin-side down until golden brown. (No need to fry the other side.) Take from the pan and place on a plate.

Fry the courgette (if using) in the pan until lightly browned, then add the garlic along with the sliced fresh red peppers or the frozen pieces. Add the olives (and capers if using in place of courgette), basil or pesto, dried herbs, chilli and paprika and finally the tomatoes. Give everything a good stir then add back the chicken, skin-side up.

Preheat the oven to 200°C/180°C fan/400°F/gas 6 and cook for 1 hour either in the ovenproof frying pan or casserole with a lid, in a pressure cooker for 20 minutes on High, or in the slow cooker for 4–5 hours. Alternatively, you can place the frying pan with the lid on the hob, bring to the boil, turn down and simmer very gently for 40–50 minutes. After 30 minutes remove the lid and allow to bubble gently to reduce the sauce if it needs to be thicker.

Serve with a garnish of fresh basil leaves and, if you have them, potatoes and a green vegetable, or on a bed of pasta.

The Four Breasts
CHICKEN KYIV
SERVES 4

Chicken Kyiv is one of my favourite 'fast and convenient' foods and the handy plastic packs containing two highly processed 'Kyivs' used to be a go-to, I have to say. Inexpensive, easy to cook, covered in a thickened layer of breadcrumbs and oozing out hot butter (maybe butter), flavoured with garlic and herbs. What's not to like?

Once again, I asked myself why I was buying these – is it because I like the taste and they are convenient? They are not difficult to make at home, pop into the freezer then cook from frozen just like the mass-produced versions. Only this time, it really is a chicken breast, it really is butter, real herbs and garlic – and they taste so much better than the mass-produced alternatives.

4 chicken breasts
80g room-temperature butter
4 tbsp chopped fresh herbs, or 2 tbsp dried
About 100g home-made Golden Breadcrumbs (page 14)
Salt and pepper
Spray oil (make your own, page 216)

You will need:
Sharp knife
Chopping board
2 small bowls
Teaspoon
Air fryer or baking tray

TIP
For variety you can add different flavours to the butter, such as 4 tbsp finely chopped fresh wild garlic with 1 crushed clove of garlic, or combine garlic and chives or cheese and chives.

Using a sharp knife, make a pocket in the side of each chicken breast – the thinnest side of each breast. Go in fairly deep to about halfway across. Wiggle the knife from side to side to make a hole for the flavoured butter.

In the small bowl mix together the very soft butter with the herbs and some salt and pepper. For each Kyiv I use a heaped teaspoon of flavoured butter and pop this into the pocket using the teaspoon. Squeeze the chicken breast together using both hands then set aside on a plate.

I have found there is no need to dip the chicken in egg before the breadcrumbs, as the meat is sufficiently moist that the breadcrumbs will easily adhere. Tip the breadcrumbs into a bowl then roll the chicken breast around in the breadcrumbs using your hands until all covered. Transfer to a plate, cover and chill until ready to cook. You can also freeze them at this point on the plate then pack into a bag once solid.

To cook, spray both sides with oil then air-fry for 15–20 minutes or oven cook on a baking tray for 20–25 minutes at 200°C/180°C fan/400°F/gas 6. The chicken will be cooked through and the flavoured butter will be oozing out.

The Four Breasts
A QUICK & EASY CURRY
SERVES 4–6

I enjoy a curry and would never try to emulate the curry experts, but if you want something fast, simple and tasty with not too many ingredients, read on. I have curry cookbooks yet I find that often when I look at a recipe I am never able to quite put my hands on all of the ingredients, and by the time I have read the recipe I can feel quite exhausted – and this is before I start the cooking. I live in a fairly small town, and sourcing some of the ingredients results in me having to go online to buy a pack of this or that, never to be used again.

This curry is quick, easy and, more importantly, made from scratch. No highly processed cooking sauces or jars, just a simple list of ingredients, short cooking time in the oven or on the hob and it is utterly delicious.

1 tbsp oil
2 medium onions,
    thinly sliced
2 tsp cumin seeds
Zest and juice of 1 lime
30g bunch of fresh
    coriander, chopped
1–2 tsp salt
2–3 garlic cloves, sliced
4 tbsp medium
    curry powder
4 chicken breasts
    (about 800g), cut into
    5cm (2 inch) chunks
4 tbsp plain yoghurt
400ml tin of coconut milk
4 tbsp tomato puree

Optional extras, if to hand:
1 green pepper,
    deseeded and sliced
2 spring onions, chopped
Fresh red chilli, sliced

You will need:
Chopping board and knife
Measuring spoons
Medium-sized casserole
    dish or large saucepan
Wooden spoon

Heat the oil in the saucepan, then fry the onions in the hot oil over a medium heat until the edges begin to brown. Turn down the heat then add the cumin seeds plus the lime zest and juice. Add half the coriander to the onions – I include the stalks in here too, reserving the half containing mostly leaves for later. Add the salt, garlic and curry powder. Stir everything together then add the chunks of chicken and the yoghurt. Stir until the chicken is well coated in the yoghurt and seasonings then add the coconut milk and tomato puree.

If using any of the extras, add the green pepper or spring onions at this time. Give the whole lot a good stir, bring to the boil then turn down and simmer gently for 30–40 minutes uncovered, either in the oven at 210°C/190°C fan/425°F/gas 7 or on the hob.

Take from the oven, stir and check the seasoning, adding more salt if necessary. Stir the remaining coriander into the curry along with a thinly sliced fresh red chilli, if using. Serve with boiled rice.

Carcass One
COQ AU LEEKIE BEAN STEW
SERVES 4–6

This is more of a wholesome stew than a soup and I like to serve it piping hot with a loaf of fresh bread in the centre of the table. A rustic warming plate of good food. I use dried beans in this recipe – I save beans from the garden, dry them in their pods and store for winter use. If you are buying beans, dried beans are cheaper than tinned.

150g dried haricot beans,
   cannellini beans or
   white butter beans
1 tbsp oil
Raw chicken carcass
600g leeks (or use half
   leeks and half onions),
   washed and sliced
2 celery sticks, sliced
2 tsp salt
1 tbsp dried mixed herbs
   or 2–3 tbsp fresh herbs
   (parsley, thyme, sage, bay)
2 tbsp cornflour mixed
   to a thin paste with
   4 tbsp cold water
1 cup frozen peas, thawed
3 tbsp double or
   single cream

You will need:
Digital weighing scales
Small bowl
Measuring jug
Large ovenproof casserole
   dish, slow cooker or
   pressure cooker
Digital weighing scales
2 wooden spoons
   or kitchen tongs
Chopping board
Knife
Colander or metal sieve

Start the night before by adding the dried beans to a small bowl and filling it to the brim with cold water. Overnight the beans will absorb the water and will be plumped up, double their size and ready for cooking.

The next day, heat the oil in the casserole dish, the pot of a pressure cooker or slow cooker, then add the raw carcass. Use the kitchen tongs or two spoons to move the carcass around so that it browns evenly on all sides. Add the sliced leeks (and onions, if using), celery, any chicken pieces that may have come about during the jointing of the bird, salt and herbs.

Drain the beans and rinse under the cold tap, then transfer to the pan with 1 litre of cold water and cook in the pressure cooker on High for 20 minutes, in the slow cooker for 4–6 hours or in the oven at 200°C/180°C fan/400°F/gas 6 for 2–3 hours.

When the beans are cooked and the vegetables are tender, have a dish or bowl handy because you need to use the kitchen tongs to remove the carcass from the pan. Scrape off any pieces of meat that are still clinging onto the bones – the carcass may collapse but the bones are easily fished out.

Once the bones are out of the delicious stew, give it a stir, then add the cornflour paste, stir again and the stew will thicken. Add the cup of peas, stir through the cream, then taste and check the seasoning.

FAMILY PUDDINGS

These are recipes that I've found very handy over the years when feeding my own family, and I hope yours like them too.

TWO-INGREDIENT CHOCOLATE POTS

SERVES 4-6

This is one of those recipes that seems too good to be true – and it is a vegan-pleaser, too!
I grow apples and store them over winter. By late spring the apples are looking a bit wrinkled and tired, but they are perfect for this recipe. Similarly, apples that have been sitting in the fruit bowl for some time that are looking a bit dry and dull but will also be very sweet are perfect, as it means no additional sugar is needed in this recipe.

400g dessert apples
  (peeled and trimmed
  weight), cut into 5cm
  (2 inch) chunks
2 tbsp water
125g dark chocolate,
  50–70% cocoa (vegan)
Fresh raspberries
  and mint leaves, to
  decorate (optional)

You will need:
Small saucepan with lid
  or microwave-safe bowl
  and plate to cover
Stick blender
Large knife and
  chopping board
Measuring spoons
Digital weighing scales
6 small or 4 large
  ramekin dishes

Place the apples into a microwave-safe bowl. Add the water then cover the bowl with a plate and microwave on High for 3–4 minutes or until the apples have cooked down to a soft pulp. Alternatively, place the apples and water into a medium saucepan and cook over a low heat with a lid on until the apples have cooked and softened.

While the apples are cooking, chop the chocolate into very small shards. Transfer the chocolate to the hot apple puree, stir, then use a stick blender to blitz the two ingredients together. The tiny chocolate pieces will readily dissolve into the apple. The resulting mix needs to be completely smooth.

While still hot, pour into the ramekin dishes then transfer to the fridge and chill for at least 2 hours. I have kept these chocolate pots for up to 4 days in the fridge.

Serve chilled, garnished with fresh raspberries and mint, if you like.

PANCAKES

MAKES 12

I don't think I know anyone that doesn't love pancakes, yet I used to only make them once a year on Shrove Tuesday (pancake day), unlike the French, whose crêpes can be found on many a menu at any time. They can be served up with a savoury filling as well as sweet – the possibilities are endless.

My recipe introduces a little melted butter into the batter which enhances the flavour and also helps to prevent sticking.

100g plain flour
Pinch of salt
2 large eggs
350ml whole milk
60g butter
Vegetable oil, for frying
Sugar, lemon zest or juice,
   maple or golden syrup
   or fruit, to serve

You will need:
Digital weighing scales
Mixing bowl
Fork
Measuring jug
Small saucepan
Small frying pan –
   20cm (8 inch)
Ladle
Fish slice to turn
   (or flip!)

In a roomy mixing bowl, place the flour and salt, then make a well in the middle. Crack 1 egg into the well and stir briskly with a fork, bringing in the flour gradually as you go. Repeat with the other egg. By mixing them in this way you will avoid lumps. When the eggs have been incorporated and you have a thick mixture, start to add the milk, a little at a time, until the mixture has fully loosened, then add the rest.

In a small saucepan, melt the butter and allow it to foam, then just at the point it starts to brown, take it off the heat and pour it into your bowl of batter. Mix well then leave to stand until you are ready to start cooking. If you plan to cook the pancakes later, place the bowl in the fridge for up to 6 hours.

In a frying pan, add about 1 teaspoon of vegetable oil, and when it is really hot pop in a measure of batter. Your first pancake will always be a trial one to understand the heat of the pan, the amount of mixture and the cooking time. Your mixture should just reach the edges of the pan and not have a puddle left in the middle. If you don't put enough into the pan then you will not have enough mixture to achieve a round pancake. Cook for 40–60 seconds on each side for a golden brown, delicious-looking pancake. Flip over using just the pan if you have the confidence, but I use a fish slice to quickly turn it over. Continue until you have used all the batter.

Pancakes will keep warm if popped onto a warm plate then covered with a tea towel between each frying.

Serve with sugar and lemon juice or a savoury filling if you prefer. I like them with fresh fruit, maple syrup and a zesting of lemon.

BUDGET STEAMED SPONGE PUDDING

SERVES 4–6

On the coldest of days, when the family come home needing something warm, comforting and filling, a light and lovely sponge pudding can just hit the spot. I am sure this must be the quickest, easiest and cheapest sponge pudding ever – and you will know exactly what has gone into making it. There's no need to reach for the overpriced supermarket packaged alternatives with a sell-by date that is way into the future. Check the ingredients list, too, and resist the ultra-processed factory-produced versions – you can make and bake a superb sponge for four people in minutes! The recipe below is for a Cranberry and Orange pudding (a favourite after Christmas when I use up leftover cranberry sauce), but I've included some flavour variations here, too.

3 tbsp cranberry sauce
100g room-temperature
   butter
100g sugar (granulated
   or caster)
120g self-raising flour
Finely grated zest and
   juice of 1 small orange
1 large egg

You will need:
Greaseproof paper
Pencil and scissors
450g (1lb) microwave-
   safe pudding basin,
   greased or brushed with
   Lining Paste (page 86)
Mixing bowl
Hand-held electric whisk
Spatula
Digital weighing scales
Zester
Plate
Microwave
Oven gloves

Turn the basin upside down and mould a small piece of greaseproof paper around and over the base. Cut into a neat circle so that the paper just covers the base and comes about 1cm (½ inch) up the side. Turn the basin the right way around, then brush with lining paste or grease with butter. Pop the piece of greaseproof paper in the base – it should fit snugly and just be touching the sides of the basin.

Add the cranberry sauce to the base of the basin.

In the mixing bowl, add all of the remaining ingredients and mix well with the electric whisk to a smooth creamy batter. Spoon this over the cranberry sauce, then smooth off the top with the back of a spoon or spatula. Cover with a microwave-safe plate turned upside down over the basin.

Pop into the microwave and cook on High for 3½ minutes (my oven is 1000w – adjust to 4 minutes for 900w and 5 minutes for 800w), then rest for 1 minute (simply leave the bowl in the microwave with no power).

Remove from the microwave and, with gloved hands, flip the whole lot over so that the pudding is now inverted onto the plate. Carefully lift the bowl off the pudding. The greaseproof paper ensures that no fruit, jam or cranberry sauce is left behind in the bowl. Peel the paper off carefully and enjoy this light yet comforting pudding hot, with cream or custard.

Recipe continued overleaf

If you don't have a
microwave, the pudding
can be 'steamed' in the
oven. Place the pudding
in a large saucepan or
casserole dish with a
well-fitting lid. Pour
sufficient boiling water
into the pan to come
about one-third of
the way up the bowl
inside the casserole.
Put the lid on and
place in the oven at
200°C/180°C fan/400°F/
gas 6, or the top oven of
the Aga for 50 minutes.

Remove the dish
from the oven and let
the pudding sit for at
least 20 minutes – it
won't spoil in this time
provided the lid is not
taken off the pan.

VARIATIONS:

Lemon Sponge Pudding: Add 3 tablespoons lemon curd
to the base of the bowl and add the grated zest and juice
of 1 lemon in place of the orange.

Steamed Treacle Sponge: Add 3 tablespoons golden syrup
to the base of the bowl and 1 teaspoon vanilla extract and
3 tablespoons milk to the mix in place of the orange.

Quick Spotted Dick: Don't add anything to the bottom
of the basin (though I still line with a circle of paper to
ensure 'easy out'.) Peel and grate 1 small apple – preferably
an overripe one – add 1 teaspoon ground cinnamon and
30g currants and stir thoroughly into the whisked-up
pudding batter.

FLEXI STICKY TOFFEE PUDDING

SERVES 8

A popular pudding that's so often seen on restaurant and pub menus, and it is well up there with the 'ready meal' list of sweets and desserts in the supermarket. We can turn our back on all of that packaging and extra cost by using simple ingredients to make something at home that tastes better than the mass-produced versions.

This is a truly comforting pudding, and what I really like about this recipe is that the puddings freeze well, as does the sauce, so you can make a batch, eat two portions (or however many you need for one sitting), then freeze the rest. Then, when you next want a quick pudding, it's out of the freezer and into the microwave for 1–2 minutes – both pudding and sauce – and you have an instant pud! Chopped dates give the best flavour here, but you can also use home-preserved or shop-bought dried plums, prunes, raisins or sultanas. This recipe is very flexible and can be baked in the oven, microwave or a multi-cooker using the Bake setting. Serve with a scoop of Vanilla Ice Cream (page 214).

For the pudding:
170g chopped dates
    or other dried fruit
2 tsp Vanilla Extract
    (page 213)
1 tbsp golden syrup
1 tbsp black treacle
90g room-temperature
    butter
90g sugar
170g self-raising flour
2 large eggs

For the caramel sauce:
100ml single cream
120g soft brown sugar
120g salted butter,
    cut into cubes
½ tsp salt (optional,
    for extra salt taste)

Start by preparing the fruit mix. In a small heatproof mixing bowl place the dried fruits then add the vanilla, golden syrup and black treacle. Pour over 200ml of boiling water and leave to soak for at least 15 minutes until the mixture is cool and the fruits have softened and can be mashed with a fork or stick blender to a thick but fairly rough puree.

To make the puddings simply place the butter, sugar, flour, eggs and pureed fruit mix into a roomy mixing bowl, and using a hand-held electric whisk, mix until the mixture is well combined and no white flecks of flour show through in the batter.

Divide evenly among the 8 prepared pudding tins (I find an ice-cream scoop handy to do this evenly), or transfer the batter to the tin or microwave-proof bowl of choice and prepare to flexi-bake as follows.

To cook in the oven, place the individual tinned puddings on a baking sheet and bake for 18–20 minutes at 180°C/160°C fan/350°F/gas 4 until risen and springy to the touch.

Recipe continued overleaf

8 x 150ml mini pudding tins, or 1 x 18cm (7 inch) square tin or 1 x 20cm (8 inch) round tin, 5cm (2 inches) deep, microwave-safe if cooking in the microwave, and well greased or brushed with Dark Lining Paste (see Tip below)
Digital weighing scales
Small mixing bowl
Mixing bowl
Spatula
Hand-held electric whisk
Stick blender or fork
Ice-cream scoop
Cooling rack
Mixing jug
Small saucepan

TIP
Leftover portions can be frozen for up to 3 months or covered and chilled for up to 5 days and quickly reheated in the microwave.

TIP
Dark lining paste ensures no white streaks on dark bakes such as chocolate cakes, coffee cakes, Jamaican-style ginger cake (page 102).
    Whisk together 50g butter, 40g plain flour, 10g cocoa powder and 50ml vegetable oil – keep in a jar in the fridge.

If you are serving the puddings immediately, simply pop the tins upside down into your pudding bowl – the tins will just lift off. The puddings are served upside down. Alternatively, turn the puddings out of the tin and leave on a cooling rack to go completely cold, then freeze.

To cook in the microwave, cover the microwave-safe dish with a plate or plastic bowl and microwave on High for 4 minutes, rest for 1 minute, then microwave for a further 2 minutes. Leave to stand for 2 minutes before serving. Microwaves vary, so check to make sure the centre of the pudding is cooked by inserting a wooden cocktail stick. If the stick comes out clean the pudding is well baked, if there is any uncooked batter, microwave a further 2 minutes.

To cook in the multi-cooker, select the Bake setting and a temperature of 150°C, preheating for 5 minutes before adding the pudding. Bake for 50 minutes, again, checking to make sure the pudding is baked using the cocktail stick as above.

While the puddings are baking make the sauce. Place the cream and sugar in a small saucepan and heat gently until the sugar dissolves. Bring to a fast boil then turn off the heat. Add the cubed butter and stir until it melts. The sauce will be smooth, silky and shiny and perfect consistency for pouring over your puddings. The sauce can be made well ahead and reheated.

To cook the sauce in the microwave, add all of the ingredients to a 1-litre microwave-safe jug, then microwave on High for 30 seconds, stir, then microwave for another 30 seconds or until the sauce is thick, silky and smooth. If you want to make a salted caramel sauce simply add the salt at the beginning of the cooking.

Serve a warm pudding with the sauce over and a scoop of vanilla ice cream. A winner!!

LEMON DELICIOUS PUDDING

SERVES 4–6

This pudding is so simple, needs very few ingredients, can be prepared ahead, is easily adapted to be gluten-free, and everyone loves it. Light, zesty and melt in the mouth with a thin, crispy crust, you can serve this either hot or chilled. I prefer it hot with Vanilla Ice Cream (page 214).

75g plain flour or
  gluten-free plain flour
Finely grated zest
  and juice of 2 lemons
250ml whole milk
100g room-temperature
  butter
100g sugar (caster
  or granulated)
3 large eggs, separated
Icing sugar, for dusting

You will need:
Ovenproof dish
  (mine measures
  20 x 16 x 5cm /
  8 x 6 x 2 inches),
  greased well or use
  Lining Paste (page 86)
Hand-held electric whisk
2 large mixing bowls
Small bowl
Lemon zester
Spoon or spatula
Measuring jug
Digital weighing scales

Add the flour to the small bowl and add the lemon zest.

Measure the milk into a jug, stir in the lemon juice and set aside. It will curdle and thicken.

In one of the large mixing bowls, cream together the butter and sugar with the hand-held electric whisk until creamy and fluffy in texture. Add the egg yolks, one at a time, to the creamed butter and sugar, whisking well between each addition. Add the flour and lemon zest mix and whisk to incorporate. The mixture will be thick in texture. Next add the thickened milk a little at a time until all of the milk has been added and the batter is thin and smooth.

If you want to get ahead the mixture can be left in this state in the fridge for several hours. Leave the bowl of egg whites at room temperature.

When ready to assemble and bake, preheat the oven to 200°C/180°C fan/400°F/gas 6.

Using clean whisks, whip the egg whites until they are at the stiff peak stage. Take the lemon batter, give it a stir then start to fold in the whisked egg whites. Use a large spoon and fold them in in three sessions. Don't whisk them in – you want to keep as much air as possible in the mix. The mixture may appear a little lumpy, but this is fine. Transfer the batter to the buttered dish and bake for 35–40 minutes. The pudding will be golden brown on the top.

Sift over a dusting of icing sugar and serve at the table straight from the dish. Any leftover pudding is also delicious chilled the next day.

SEASONS & CELEBRATIONS

I want this book to be very much a handy piece of kit – one you can turn to most days. The market is saturated with cookery books to suit every occasion, every cooking appliance and which feature everything from top-end patisserie to low-fat and low-calorie foods.

I think most of us gather a number of recipes that are enjoyed, that work and that can be brought out to fit the bill when entertaining or on holidays and times of celebration.

I include a selection of my 'go-to' recipes here. I have chosen them because most of all they are tasty. I try to use a few easily accessible ingredients so they don't come with an expensive price tag and with a little attention to detail they can look good too!

TWO-SALMON PLAIT

SERVES 8

Perfect for sharing, hot or cold – this is SO tasty. Choose fresh, previously unfrozen salmon if your plan is to freeze the plait. This can be made a day ahead and baked from chilled, or frozen after egg washing and then baked from frozen. I make this over and over again for friends and family whatever the season – it goes a long way and is a fantastic crowd-pleaser.
*   Serve cold with salads or hot with potatoes and vegetables – you will not be disappointed.*

500–700g skinless
   salmon fillet
1–2 tsp sea salt
1–2 tsp freshly ground
   black pepper
4 tbsp finely chopped
   fresh dill
Flour, for dusting
500g Hands-Free Puff
   Pastry (page 211)
120g smoked salmon
   (4 slices)
150g full-fat soft cheese
Finely grated zest
   of 1 lime
2 tbsp finely
   chopped chives
1 large egg, separated

You will need:
Kitchen paper
Chopping board
   and knife
Measuring spoons
Rolling pin
Tape measure or ruler
Pizza cutter
Bowl
Zester
Reusable piping bag
Pastry brush
2 baking sheets – one
   lined with reusable
   baking parchment
Temperature probe

Start by preparing the salmon fillet. Dry on kitchen paper then trim to make an even oblong shape, reserving the offcuts. Season both sides with salt and pepper then cover the top side of the fillet with the finely chopped dill. Set aside.

On a lightly floured work surface, roll out the puff pastry to an oblong measuring roughly 28 x 38cm (11 x 15 inches). Neaten the edges with a pizza cutter then transfer to a baking sheet lined with baking parchment. With the pastry piece in front of you (portrait style) score two lines so that the pastry is marked into thirds, but don't cut all the way through – these lines are simply to guide.

Lay two slices of smoked salmon side by side down the centre panel of the pastry piece, allowing a 3cm (1 inch) margin top and bottom, then lay the dill-coated salmon fillet on top. Use any salmon offcuts to pack side by side at the base of the plait in order to maintain an oblong shape.

Mix together the soft cheese, lime zest and chopped chives, then spread over the top of the salmon fillet (I find it easiest to use a piping bag for this). Use the remaining two slices of smoked salmon to cover the cream cheese.

Recipe continued overleaf

To make the plait, cut regularly-spaced strips in the two pieces of pastry either side of the fillet then, starting at the top, fold down the 3cm (1 inch) top and then fold one strip over the other, working from side to side and securing and gluing using the pastry brush dipped in the egg white.

Once down to the bottom of the pastry, fold up the 3cm (1 inch) piece of pastry before covering with the strips. Chill for at least 1 hour to allow everything to firm up.

Brush over a wash of egg yolk mixed with 1 teaspoon water, then chill for a further half hour.

The salmon plait can be frozen at this stage. After chilling, apply a second egg wash and then freeze. Bake from frozen (see Tip).

When ready to bake, preheat the oven to 200°C/180°C fan/ 400°F/gas 6 and place a baking sheet inside to heat. Take the plait from the fridge and apply another egg wash before sliding it from the chilled baking sheet to the preheated one. This will ensure the pastry seals immediately at the base so there's no soggy bottom. Bake for 30–40 minutes until dark golden. Remove from the oven and allow to stand for 5 minutes before slicing and serving.

SERVE UP A SAVOURY SOUFFLE

SERVES 6

If you believe that souffles are dangerous things to make because they have to be served immediately, can disappointingly sink and are an awful lot of effort, try this recipe!

These individual souffles are made in advance, can be chilled, even frozen and reheated when required – they are packed with flavour, light and perfect for a celebration starter when you want to show off to your friends. Use cornflour in place of the plain flour and your recipe becomes gluten-free!

These souffles are the perfect start to a meal – small, tasty and you can use any selection of greens and cheese. Leeks, spinach and Swiss chard work exceptionally well. For this recipe I have used kale and strong Cheddar cheese, though any hard cheese works beautifully. The stronger the flavour, the better – try a blue cheese!

60–80g kale (trimmed weight – no stalks)
220ml whole milk
1 bay leaf
1 small onion, cut in half
6 black peppercorns
Grating of nutmeg
40g butter
40g plain flour or cornflour
150g strong Cheddar cheese, roughly grated, plus 30g strong Cheddar cheese, finely diced
4 large eggs, separated
Salt and pepper
3 tbsp finely chopped chives or parsley, to garnish
A few salad leaves and cherry tomatoes, cut in half, to serve (optional)

Start by cooking the kale or other green vegetable because it needs to be cooked and cooled before using – you can do this the day before if you prefer. Boil the kale in a little salted water until just tender (about 5 minutes), then drain and plunge immediately into a bowl of cold water to stop the cooking and at the same time hold onto the vivid green colour. Strain in a colander then squeeze out surplus water using your hands and dry on kitchen paper or a clean tea towel. Chop into small pieces then set aside.

In a small saucepan heat the milk, bay leaf, onion, peppercorns and nutmeg to simmering point, then remove from the heat and strain the seasoned milk into a heatproof jug. Discard the onion and other flavourings.

In the same small saucepan (it saves on the washing up), melt the butter over a medium heat then stir in the flour or cornflour and add the strained cooled milk little by little, stirring, to avoid lumps. Once all of the milk has been added, continue to stir over a low heat with a whisk until a thick, smooth paste forms.

Recipe continued overleaf

You will need:
Saucepan with lid
Colander
Small saucepan
Chopping board
    and knife
2 mixing bowls
Jug
Strainer or sieve
Whisk
Wooden spoon or fork
Hand-held electric whisk
6 ramekins – mine
    measure 7.5cm
    (3 inches) in diameter
    x 4cm (1½ inches) deep,
    well greased or use
    Lining Paste (page 86)
Roasting tin which will
    fit your six ramekins
Cooling rack
Baking sheet lined
    with reusable
    baking parchment

Take from the heat and transfer the thick paste into a large mixing bowl. Add the grated cheese and the cold chopped kale. Add the egg yolks one at a time, stirring well between each addition – I use a wooden spoon or fork. Set aside.

Preheat the oven to 200°C/180°C fan/400°F/gas 6.

In the large clean bowl, whisk the egg whites until soft peaks are formed. I use a hand-held electric whisk for this – it will take 3–4 minutes. The whites will look thick, smooth, shiny and will almost half-fill the bowl. Take a large spoonful of whisked egg white and fold it into the main mix in the other bowl – this will loosen it slightly, making it more liquid. The remaining egg whites can be transferred to the main mix and the two mixtures can be folded together gently. They will come together easily without losing all of the valuable air that will ensure the souffles rise!

Season the mix generously with salt and pepper then divide evenly among the 6 prepared ramekins using a large spoon. Fill the ramekins right to the top. Transfer the ramekins to the roasting tin and pour some recently boiled water into the tin, allowing it to come about halfway up the ramekin dishes. Transfer to the oven and bake for 20 minutes until the souffles are beautifully risen, golden and smelling absolutely divine.

Take from the oven and immediately remove them from the water bath using gloved hands, then place onto a cooling rack and leave to go completely cold. The souffles will have lost their rise but don't worry it will come back when they are reheated.

Take a knife and run it around the edge of each ramekin dish before turning the soufflés out onto a baking sheet. The souffles can now be chilled for up to 24 hours or frozen for up to 3 months.

When ready to complete the cooking, preheat the oven to 200°C/180°C fan/400°F/gas 6. Top the cold souffles with the finely diced cheese then pop into the oven on a baking sheet for 25 minutes (35 minutes from frozen) until the souffles are once again risen and the cheese is bubbling on the top.

Serve immediately on small plates, garnished with chopped chives or parsley, with a few salad leaves and cherry tomatoes.

ECCLES CAKES

MAKES 9–10

It is said that when Oliver Cromwell gained power in 1650 AD, both festival wakes and the eating of Eccles cakes were banned due to the Puritan belief that they had pagan connections. Centuries later and these two celebrations are still going strong. I remember enjoying an Eccles cake with coffee at work in my first ever job, over 50 years ago.

Supermarkets will sell mass-produced version of these cakes, but nothing tastes as good as home-made – with the added bonus that you can adjust additional flavours to suit your own family's taste.

This recipe is simple yet delicious and I often make a few with leftover puff pastry. Enjoy while still warm and slightly sticky, or cold with tea and coffee – a wedge of hard British cheese is also a great accompaniment.

This recipe makes 9–10 but you can easily scale it down if you don't have enough leftover pastry dough.

80g currants (or use whatever dried fruits you have)
10g caster sugar
½ tsp Vanilla Extract (page 213) or ½ tsp mixed spice, ground cinnamon or nutmeg
80ml boiling water (or 25ml elderflower cordial and 55ml boiling water)
250g puff pastry (page 211)
Flour, for dusting
Milk wash and granulated or demerara sugar, for glazing

Put the currants, sugar and vanilla in a small heatproof bowl, then pour over the boiling water. Alternatively, for a fruity filling, leave out the vanilla and sugar, and pour the elderflower cordial and boiling water over the currants. For a spicy cake, add ½ teaspoon of mixed spice, cinnamon or nutmeg to the fruits and pour over boiling water and the sugar. Whichever version you choose, set aside to allow the currants to plump up and absorb the liquid. I leave mine overnight where possible, but a couple of hours or until the water cools is fine.

Roll out the pastry very thinly on a lightly floured work surface and cut out 9–10 circles using a 10cm (4 inch) cutter, rerolling the trimmings as you go.

Place a heaped teaspoon of the cold currant mixture into the centre of each circle, draw the pastry edges together to form a purse, dampening the edges slightly if you find it necessary, though the pastry should adhere together without. I find the fat in the pastry along with a little heat from the hands will be enough to help the little purses to seal.

Recipe continued overleaf

Digital weighing scales
Measuring jug
Measuring spoons
Small heatproof bowl
Rolling pin
10cm (4 inch) cutter
Pastry brush
Small pizza cutter,
  blade or pointed knife
Baking sheet lined
  with reusable
  baking parchment

On a floured surface (or directly onto the lined baking sheet), turn the pastry parcels upside down with the joins to the bottom, then lightly roll the upper side, forming a circle and allowing the currants just to show under the surface.

Preheat the oven to 220°C/200°C fan/425°F/gas 7. Chill until the oven comes to temperature.

Brush with milk then sprinkle with granulated or demerara sugar. Using a pizza cutter, blade or sharp pointed knife, make 3 slashes on each cake. Bake in a hot oven for 15–20 minutes until the cakes are dark golden brown, gooey and bubbling.

MINI SIMNEL CAKES

MAKES 9 MINI CAKES OR 1 LARGE CAKE

Who doesn't love spring? The longer days, colour in the garden and hedgerows, birds singing, warmer weather, sunshine and the Easter holiday usually springs all of us into action. Many families have their own Easter traditions and I see nowadays there is a tendency for shops to fill windows and shelves with an array of Easter-themed plastic decorations, flowers, cards, chocolate eggs and sweets in such abundance that I really thought I must be missing something.

Throughout my childhood and even my early adult life when I had young children of my own, Easter was still a happy time, which included going to church – for which the gift was a chocolate egg – and my grandma would have baked a Simnel cake. That was it – oh, hang on a minute, also one year we decorated hard-boiled eggs and I was allowed to pick daffodils from the garden.

Lighter and fresher than Christmas cake, the Simnel cake is a classic Easter bake and one that I adore. Before it became an established Easter celebration cake, this used to be made by girls in service to gift on Mothering Sunday. I read that the lady of the house would take the opportunity to showcase her quality ingredients to the family of her servant who would have been given the one day off on Mothering Sunday to travel home to visit her mother.

If you don't want to be sucked into the hefty, plastic-packaged, expensive Easter-gift-buying frenzy, a home-made, beautiful, mini Simnel cake will put a smile on anyone's face.

440g mixed dried fruits (currants, sultanas, raisins and mixed peel)

Finely grated zest and juice of 2 large lemons (or 3 small)

275g butter

240g sugar

4 large eggs

50ml milk

330g plain flour

2½ tsp mixed spice

Pinch of salt

1 tsp baking powder

120g ready-to-eat apricots, cut into small dice

160g glacé cherries, halved, washed, dried and dusted in 1 tbsp of the flour

The day before you want to bake the cake, place the dried mixed fruits into a bowl, add the finely grated lemon zest plus the juice, then cover and leave to soak in a cool place overnight.

When ready to bake, cream together the butter and sugar in a bowl with the hand-held electric whisk until light and fluffy. Add the eggs one at a time, whisking well between each addition, then add the milk. Mix together the flour, spice, salt and baking powder then sift this over the creamed batter and mix well. Add the soaked fruits and juice, apricots and cherries and stir until well combined.

Preheat the oven to 100°C/80°C fan/210°F/gas ¼.

I find an ice-cream scoop is useful to divide the cake batter evenly among the tins. A good scoop of batter needs to weigh around 100g (half of the cake size). Pop this into the base of each tin and smooth out with the back of a teaspoon.

Recipe continued overleaf

500g golden marzipan
Icing sugar, for dusting
1–2 tbsp apricot jam

You will need:
Digital weighing scales
2 large mixing bowls
Grater or zester
Hand-held electric whisk
Sieve
Ice-cream scoop
9 x 7.5cm (3 inch)
    metal baking sleeves
    (or use 200g baked
    bean tins, top and
    bottom removed,
    washed) lined with
    baking parchment
    or greaseproof paper.
    A spray of oil onto the
    tin will help the paper
    to adhere to it. Stand
    the tins on a baking
    sheet or tray lined
    with greaseproof
    paper or reusable
    baking parchment.
Rolling pin
Sharp knife
Teaspoon
Temperature probe
    (optional)
Cook's blowtorch
    (optional)

Roll out half of the marzipan on a surface dusted with a little icing sugar to prevent sticking, then cut out nine 6cm (2½ inch) discs and lay them onto the cake batter. Top off with the rest of the batter, smooth the tops with the back of a teaspoon, then bake low and slow for 5 hours. The internal baked temperature of the cakes needs to be 92°C (200°F) if you have a temperature probe.

Once cooked, leave to cool in the tins then remove them by pushing from the base using a weight or the end of a rolling pin. Remove the paper then flip the cakes over to present a flat top for decorating. Spread the now-top of the cakes with a thin layer of jam.

Roll out the rest of the marzipan (including the trimmings from the previous rolling) and cut out nine 7.5cm (3 inch) rounds. Place on top of the cakes then decorate with 11 small balls of marzipan using the offcuts. I have a small-hole fondant cutter which ensures I have even sizes for decoration. Brush the top of the marzipan with water to help secure the decorations and toast with a cook's blowtorch if you have one.

The cakes will keep for several weeks in an airtight tin or wrapped in compostable clear wrap.

TIP
This recipe will alternatively make a 20cm (8 inch) round cake. Use a deep cake tin fully lined with greaseproof paper and extend the baking time to 10 hours – I bake from 10pm to 8am the next day. The cake can be made well in advance of Easter (at least three weeks) and will keep for at least that time in a tin.

SUMMER

BEETROOT SALAD

SERVES 2-4

*A salad that's easy to scale up for a crowd. It's easy to make ahead and looks colourful too –
it will be a vibrant dark colour with flashes of green from the chives and onions.*

100g couscous
150ml boiling water
1 tbsp cumin seeds,
    toasted and crushed
70g silverskin onions
    or 2–3 spring onions,
    finely chopped
400g cooked beetroot,
    cut into small dice
Bunch of fresh chives,
    finely chopped
Zest of ½ lemon
2 tbsp olive oil
Salt and pepper

You will need:
Large heatproof bowl
Digital weighing scales
Measuring spoons
Knife and chopping
    board

Start by placing the couscous in a large roomy bowl and pour
over the boiling water. Cover and leave until the couscous
has absorbed the water and gone completely cold.

Fluff up with a fork then simply add all the remaining
ingredients. Give a good stir, cover and leave in the fridge
to develop – the couscous will absorb the juices from the
beetroot. This will keep in the fridge for 3 days.

FRESH TOMATO SALAD

SERVES 6-8

I have absolutely no idea where I got this recipe, I only know I have been making this salad for many, many years. It complements my Quick and Easy Curry (page 136) beautifully.

600g cherry tomatoes,
  cut in half
1 whole cucumber, cut
  into 1cm (½inch) dice
Bunch of spring onions
  chopped into 5mm
  (¼ inch) pieces
Grated zest of 1 lemon
2 tsp mint sauce
3 tbsp lemon juice
2 tbsp chopped
  coriander leaves
Salt, to taste

You will need:
Knife and chopping
  board
Bowl
Grater
Measuring spoons

Put all the ingredients together in a bowl, stir and serve.

Alternatively, if you want to prepare in advance, put the tomatoes, cucumber, spring onions and zest into a bowl and stir. In another bowl, mix the mint sauce, salt (to taste) and lemon juice. Cover and leave in the fridge. Just before serving, give the whole lot a good stir to incorporate the lemon juice, salt and mint sauce. Sprinkle the coriander leaves over.

STRAWBERRIES & CREAM ROULADE

SERVES 6-8

In the summer months this simple bake can become a super showstopper, filled with fresh cream and strawberries then coated in a white chocolate ganache and decorated with strawberries.

For the ganache:
200g white chocolate,
    broken into pieces
200ml double cream

For the Swiss roll:
3 large eggs
75g caster sugar
1 tsp Vanilla Extract
    (page 213)
75g plain flour, sifted

For the filling:
250ml double cream
1 tsp icing sugar
½ tsp Vanilla Extract
    (page 213)
100g strawberries,
    chopped, plus extra
    for decoration

You will need:
Swiss roll tin or
    lipped baking tray –
    37 x 26 x 2cm
    (14 x 10 x ¾ inch)
    greased with Lining
    Paste (page 86)
Small bowl
Small saucepan
Mixing bowl
Hand-held electric whisk
Digital weighing scales
Clean tea towel
Cooling rack
Large metal spoon
Sieve
Angled palette knife
    or teaspoon
Knife

Preheat the oven to 180°C/160°C fan/350°F/gas 4 and brush the tin with lining paste or line with baking paper.

First, make the ganache. Put the chocolate pieces in the small bowl. Heat the cream in the small saucepan and once it begins to bubble at the sides (not boiling), pour it over the chocolate and leave to stand.

To make the Swiss roll sponge, refer to the instructions for Chocolate Log on pages 201–203.

While the sponge is in the oven, put the cream, icing sugar and vanilla into a large mixing bowl and whip up to soft peaks. Set aside.

Give the chocolate and cream a stir – the heat from the cream should have melted the chocolate and resulted in a thick, shiny, smooth ganache. Leave to cool further and thicken.

Take the sponge from the oven, cover with the tea towel or cloth and pop the cooling rack on top, then quickly flip the whole lot over. Lift the hot tin from the cake and peel off the paper, if used, then slide away the rack from underneath.

The sponge is now lying on the cloth. With your cake in 'portrait' position, start at one end and roll the sponge, enclosing the cloth. Don't worry if it cracks. Leave the sponge to cool, still rolled in the cloth on the cooling rack.

When ready to assemble, unroll the sponge, spread over the whipped cream using an angled palette knife or back of a teaspoon, then scatter over the chopped strawberries.

Roll up the Swiss roll, finishing with the seam underneath, then transfer to the serving plate. Spread the chocolate ganache over the Swiss roll – not forgetting the ends. Wipe any smudges from the plate, chill for an hour or so, then serve.

'SHOWSTOPPER' ANGEL FOOD CAKE

SERVES 12

This cake is wonderfully light and moist and can be 'dressed up' for any occasion.

Angel food cakes are very unusual in that the sponge is fat-free and there is no greasing of the tin. The sponge needs to cling onto the tin while baking and rising in the oven and then bizarrely when it comes out of the oven it is turned upside down to cool. This recipe also adapts well to become gluten-free – just swap in gluten-free flour in the recipe.

You will need a 23 x 10cm (9 x 4 inch) deep cake tin – not loose-bottomed. There are tins on the market which are made specifically for angel cakes that have a tube in the centre and when I saw these I considered I could easily save some money and improvise using what I already had. I needed a gin and tonic first though! I used a slim ring-pull can (250ml tonic water can) which I filled with lentils to weigh it down, then once the tin was full I plugged the hole where the ring pull was with a piece of baking paper and covered the whole tin neatly with a piece of aluminium foil. I use it over and over – leave the lentils in the tin and discard the foil cover after baking.

I always have to hand leftover egg whites that have been collecting in the freezer for this bake (page 44).

For the chocolate sponge:
190g icing sugar
100g plain flour or
    gluten-free plain flour
20g cornflour
1 tsp coffee powder
40g cocoa powder
380g egg whites at
    room temperature
    (about 10 egg whites)
1 tsp lemon juice
225g caster sugar
5g cream of tartar
1 tsp Vanilla Extract
    (page 213)

For the pastry cream:
3 egg yolks
50g caster sugar
25g cornflour
250ml milk
300ml double cream
20g icing sugar

Preheat the oven to 190°C/170°C fan/375°F/gas 5. Place a piece of baking parchment in the base of the tin and stand the tonic tin in the centre. If you have an angel food cake tin you may want to place a piece of paper in the base. Lining the base is not essential but without a piece of paper I found I left a little of the cake behind. Do not grease the sides of the tin or the can tube that is placed in the centre.

Start by sifting together the icing sugar, flour, cornflour, coffee and cocoa powder. Sift them together again, then a third time. Lots of air is required for this cake and the cocoa needs to be well incorporated. Set aside.

In a very large mixing bowl whisk together the egg whites with the lemon juice using the hand-held electric whisk until soft peaks are formed. Add then the sugar and cream of tartar, one large spoonful at a time, whisking well between each addition. You will have a very thick meringue. Fold in the flour mix in three parts, stirring slowly and thoroughly between each addition. Lastly, stir through the vanilla.

Recipe continued overleaf

1 tsp Vanilla Extract
(page 213) or
3 tbsp freeze-dried
passion fruit powder

To decorate:
300g strawberries, or any
seasonal fresh fruits

You will need:
23cm (9 inch) deep
cake tin (not loose
bottomed)
250ml slim ring-pull can
Aluminium foil
Baking parchment
Large mixing bowl
Sieve
2 medium mixing bowls
Hand-held electric whisk
Small saucepan or
microwave-safe jug
for the pastry cream
Spoon or spatula
Knife
Cooling rack

Transfer the mix to the tin and when it is all in use a knife to gently stir it around to try to settle it down and get rid of any air pockets. Pop into the oven and bake for 30 minutes.

Take from the oven and immediately turn the cake upside down onto a cooling rack. The tin inside will stand proud of the cake tin, so be careful to balance the cake carefully on the small tin. Leave the cake to go completely cold.

Once cold, turn the cake tin the right side up and run a knife around the sides and around the centre tin or tube. Remove the can from the centre first then turn out the sponge onto a rack or plate and prepare for decoration.

For the cream, put the egg yolks, sugar and cornflour in a medium-sized saucepan and mix together to a smooth paste. Gradually add the milk then place over a low heat and keep stirring until the custard thickens. Transfer to a cold bowl, cover with a plate and allow to cool completely. Alternatively, the pastry cream can be mixed in a non-metal jug and cooked in the microwave. Place the yolks, sugar and cornflour in the jug, stir well then add the milk and transfer to the microwave and cook on High for 20 seconds at a time, stirring well between each session until thickened and smooth. It will usually take 3 or 4 sessions.

Leave the pastry cream to cool completely.

When ready to mix the filling and assemble the cake, take the bowl or jug containing the cold pastry cream and add 2–3 tablespoons of the double cream and whisk the two together with the hand-held electric whisk until smooth.

In a separate bowl whisk the rest of the double cream with the icing sugar to soft peaks. Once the two consistencies are the same (the bowl of pastry cream and the double cream) they can be mixed together. Flavour with vanilla. Freeze-dried fruit powders are also handy to have in stock. I stirred passion fruit powder into mine which works very well with chocolate.

Spread the cream over the top and sides of the cake and decorate with slices of strawberry.

LEMON AND ELDERFLOWER CORDIAL

MAKES 2 LITRES

The cream coloured fragrant flowers of Elder paired with fresh lemon present one of the finest flavours in my opinion. This syrup will flavour cake fillings, fruit salads, ice creams, summer puddings and diluted with sparkling water will make the best summer non-alcoholic drink!

The end of May to the end of June is the short season to forage for elderflowers in the UK. The creamy white flowers are tiny and held in clusters and the perfume is pleasing but not as delicious as the resultant flavour of the syrup.

I make a large batch and once cool bottle into plastic bottles and place in the freezer so that I can enjoy this syrup all year long. The syrup will keep in the fridge for six weeks.

500g elderflower heads
    yielding 370g flowers
2kg granulated sugar
1.5 litres cold water
60g citric acid
2 large lemons

You will need:
Digital weighing scales
Measuring jug
Large preserving pan
    with a lid or large
    casserole dish with a lid
Vegetable peeler
Knife
Piece of fine muslin
    or jelly bag
Colander
Large saucepan
Sterilised bottles for
    storage (see page 231)

I collect my flowers in a fine mesh bag that holds onto the flowers but any bugs are able to leave the bag whilst I am out walking. Look for fresh flowers not those that are brown and beginning to fade. I do not wash the blooms, just give them a gentle tap so that any hidden bugs drop out. Cut the green stalks from the blooms, weigh the flowers and adjust the other quantities if need be.

Place the sugar in the large preserving pan or casserole dish, pour over the water and stir over a low heat until the sugar dissolves and the water is clear. Add the citric acid (which will preserve the syrup) and stir until this too dissolves in the warm water.

Pare the zest from the two lemons and add to the syrup then slice the zested fruits thinly and add them to the pan. Add in all the elderflower heads, stir and bring to the boil. Once boiling turn off the heat, give a final stir, put a lid on the pan and transfer to a cool place and leave for 24 hours.

The next day strain the syrup through a fine piece of muslin or jelly bag secured over a colander hooked over a second saucepan. Once strained, boil the syrup once more then turn off the heat. Either bottle straight away in sterilised glass bottles or leave to cool and pour into sterilised plastic bottles to be kept in the fridge for up to six weeks or freeze for a year. Allow some headroom in the plastic bottle if freezing.

Once chilled the syrup may look cloudy but just give it a shake and it will clear.

SLOW-ROAST CRISPY BELLY PORK

SERVES 6

I have to say this is one of my favourite roasts, and it's very popular on restaurant menus and in good pubs. Belly pork is unbelievably tasty; it's a less-fine cut and consequently not nearly as expensive as other joints. Ask the butcher for a single piece of belly, boned and with no scoring to the skin (but keep the bones). I marinate the piece with a herb and lemon rub then cook it low and slow for fantastic flavours and melt-in-the-mouth texture. It's perfect for entertaining as it can be made in advance and then simply browned when you are ready to serve. It can also be frozen after the long roast then defrosted before browning. Served in neat portions with a thin finger of crackling, this will have guests applauding your cookery skills.

2kg piece of belly
   pork, skin on and
   bones removed

For the marinade:
finely grated zest
   and juice of 1 lemon
2 tbsp chopped fresh
   parsley, stalks too
2 tsp fennel seeds,
   crushed
1 tbsp freshly ground
   black pepper
2 garlic cloves
2 tsp finely chopped fresh
   thyme or 1 tsp dried

For the roasting rack:
Bones from the belly
   pork or 2 carrots,
   2 small onions and
   1 celery stick (or use
   both veg and bones)

You will need:
Small blender or knife
   and chopping board
   to chop very small
Fine grater

Lay the pork skin-side down on a board or large plate. Blitz the marinade ingredients together in a blender or chop them very finely, then rub the rough paste into the flesh side of the pork belly. There will be lots of nooks and crannies to get into where the butcher has removed the bones. Cover with a sheet of greaseproof paper and place in the fridge or cold pantry for at least 6 hours, though 12 hours will be better.

I tend to cook the meat overnight, so in the late evening I take the meat from the fridge and preheat the oven to 100°C/80°C fan/210°F/gas ¼.

I then create a roasting rack from the bones by criss-crossing them on the base of the tin. If you don't have the bones, you can do the same thing with vegetables. Wash the vegetables, cut the carrots in half lengthways, then cut the onions and celery stick in half. Criss-cross the vegetables in the base of the tin to make a roasting rack for the meat.

Lay the meat skin-side uppermost on the roasting rack then pour into the tin 400ml of boiling water or sufficient to just cover the bottom of the tin and the bones/vegetables but not touch the meat. Immediately cover the meat with a lid, make a tent of foil, or use a covered roasting tin, then place in the oven and cook for 12 hours. This can be cooked in the bottom oven of the Aga or a preheated slow cooker or multi-cooker with a well-fitting lid.

Recipe continued overleaf

Oblong plate or
  sheet to fit the
  belly pork piece
Greaseproof paper
Small roasting tin
  with a cover or
  aluminium foil
Digital weighing scales
Jug
Sharp knife
Scissors
Metal fish slice
Fork

Either 12 hours later or the next morning, remove the tin from the oven or appliance and carefully place the meat, skin-side uppermost, on a flat plate or tray and allow it to go completely cold. The juices and vegetables left in the tin will be used to make a gravy.

When cold, with the sharp knife carefully remove the skin. Insert the blade of the knife just under the skin. Try to remove only the thin layer of skin, keeping it in one piece, ensuring the meat and fat are left intact. Set it aside. Trim the meat so that you have straight sides then cut it into six even-sized portions. Take the piece of skin and using scissors cut long, thin strips – these will become your crackling.

Now is the time to freeze if you need to or chill until ready to cook and serve.

When ready to make the crackling, heat a non-stick frying pan (don't add any fat or oil) on the hob, or cook in the oven, if you have an ovenproof pan, or in the air fryer. Lay the strips of skin in the pan and add a sprinkling of salt. Cover with a thin rack or trivet if you want the strips to crisp up flat, or hold them down with a metal fish slice. They tend to jump about and pop as they heat up, so beware. Turn the skin strips so that they crisp on both sides. Alternatively, let the crackling do its own thing and crisp up to the shape it does naturally – it will taste exactly the same. Once cooked and crispy, remove to a warm plate.

Reduce the heat to medium and pour off any fat before starting to brown the portions of meat. Cook each side of each portion until golden brown and heated through. Each side will take 2–3 minutes to brown – 8–10 minutes in total.

Alternatively, air-fry for 12 minutes.

The gravy can be made in advance. Discard the bones and use a fork to mash the vegetables into the juices from the pork, mix in 1–2 tablespoons of cornflour and 1 tablespoon of gravy browning with the juices from the overnight cooking. Heat and stir to thicken. Check for seasoning and add more water if the gravy is too thick. Serve with apple sauce (opposite), creamed potatoes and vegetables.

APPLE SAUCE

SERVES 6

Jars of pre-prepared apple sauce are available to buy from the supermarket and are very convenient. I have in the past grabbed a jar, transferred it into a serving bowl and popped onto the dinner table to serve alongside the pork. However, once I examined the reverse label and did a little investigation, I saw that it can often carry a red warning about its high sugar content. It is so quick and easy to make at home and a much healthier choice too – you can even add your own flavour twists if you want to experiment. Try a pinch of dried ginger or cinnamon.

3 large bramley apples (around 200–250g each or use wrinkled eating apples from the fruit bowl)
20g butter
20g sugar

You will need:
Peeler
Medium saucepan or large microwave-safe bowl with plate to cover
Spoon or fork

I prefer using the microwave to make apple sauce because there is no fear of burning the base of the pan.

Peel the apples then slice the flesh into the microwave-safe bowl as quickly as you can before the apples start to turn brown. Cover with a plate and microwave on High in 1-minute intervals until the apples soften, become fluffy and have cooked through.

While still hot stir in the butter and sugar and leave to cool.

To cook in a saucepan it's worthwhile adding 1–2 tablespoons of water or lemon juice to prevent the apple sticking to the pan. Cook over a medium heat, stirring occasionally, until the apple pieces soften and can be squashed with a fork.

I like apple sauce to be tart to offset the richness of the pork but add more sugar if you need to. I serve it at room temperature.

PEPPERED PORK WITH FRUIT: CASSEROLE VERSION

SERVES 4-6

Just as roast pork pairs well with apple sauce, the peppery sauce and fruit works well with the meat here. Delicious with new potatoes and green vegetables.

1 tsp mustard powder
¾ tsp ground black pepper
1 tsp mixed dried herbs
2 tbsp plain flour
500g lean pork, cut into
    large chunks
25g butter, 2 tbsp oil
    or 25g lard, for frying
1 large or 2 small onions,
    finely chopped
1 celery stick,
    finely chopped
2–3 garlic cloves,
    finely chopped
1 tsp salt
150ml apple juice
2 tsp vinegar
150ml water
120g tinned stoned
    prunes, drained or
    ready-to-eat apricots
1–2 tbsp fresh
    breadcrumbs
3–4 tbsp double cream
Freshly chopped parsley
    or tarragon, to garnish

You will need:
Measuring spoons
Measuring jug
Medium bowl
Casserole dish with a
    well-fitting lid, frying
    pan with a lid, slow
    cooker or multi-cooker
Wooden spoon

In the medium bowl, combine the mustard powder, pepper, dried herbs and flour. Add the chunks of pork to the bowl, coat well all over, then set aside.

Heat the fat of choice in the frying pan, casserole dish or bowl of a multi-cooker. Add the onions to the oil and cook slowly for 10 minutes or so until the onions soften. Add the celery and garlic and cook for 3–4 minutes more, stirring from time to time.

Toss in the seasoned meat, turn up the heat, and stir it around so that everything begins to take on a little caramelisation (browning) here and there. Add the salt, apple juice and vinegar (or substitute both for 160ml cider) and water. Add then the fruits of choice – I particularly like this with prunes because as well as sweetness they add a dark richness to the gravy. If using ready-to-eat apricots they can be left whole.

Stir, cover, then cook in the oven at 170°C/150°C fan/340°F/gas 4 for 45 minutes to 1 hour, in the slow cooker for 2 hours, or in the multi-cooker on 170°C for 45 minutes to 1 hour. Alternatively, you can cook it on the hob; bring to the boil, turn down to a gentle simmer and cook for 30–40 minutes until the pork is tender.

After the cooking time, check the seasoning and the thickness of the sauce. If you prefer a thicker gravy simply scatter over 1–2 tablespoons of fresh breadcrumbs (or gluten-free crumbs) and stir to instantly thicken the sauce. Pour over the cream and stir through.

Garnish with a sprinkle of freshly chopped parsley or tarragon, if you have it.

PEPPERED PORK WITH FRUIT: OVEN VERSION

SERVES 6

This is a great little recipe and I remember so many years ago serving this up to 22 people at Him Indoors' fiftieth birthday bash. I was very nervous then – and obviously a lot younger – and the pressure of getting everything served up, hot and on time while still trying to be the perfect host and seemingly being part of the party was just crazy! We have one large table but we constructed a second table from trestles and pieces of wood. Once covered and set they looked identical and we sat 10 on one and 12 on the other. It was a squeeze but lots of fun too … There was a very good 'much older than me' esteemed cook present and I remember her taking me to one side afterwards and saying 'Pork was a very brave thing to do my dear – it can be so very dry but yours wasn't.' This was praise indeed.

1 tbsp whole black
 peppercorns
6 large boneless
 pork steaks
85g butter
560g tin pineapple
 rings, drained
 and juice reserved
2 tbsp flour
6 tbsp dry sherry
1 tsp salt
12 dried apricots or
 12 dried prunes, stoned

You will need:
Pestle and mortar or
 wooden rolling pin
 and sturdy bowl
Scissors or sharp knife
Frying pan
Roasting tin large
 enough for 6 chops
Aluminium foil

TIP
Swap out the flour
for gluten-free flour
for a gluten-free option.

Crush the peppercorns using a pestle and mortar or the end of a rolling pin in a strong bowl. Trim the steaks of excess fat. Heat the butter in the frying pan and once frothing but not burning, fry the steaks in 3 batches (don't overcrowd the pan). Once browned on both sides, transfer to the roasting tin and lay them side by side.

Brown the pineapple slices in the residual fat in the pan – again, two or three at a time – and once browned lay a pineapple slice on each pork steak.

Once the pineapple slices are done, add the flour to the frying pan, stirring it around to absorb all of the juices left behind. Pour in the sherry, stirring to deglaze the pan – the alcohol will immediately evaporate – then add the reserved pineapple juice, crushed peppercorns and the salt.

Bring to the boil then pour the juice over the chops in the roasting tin (at this stage, if there looks to be insufficient liquid to cover the base of the roasting tin and almost cover the chops I may add a little extra water and sherry).

Preheat the oven to 180°C/160°C fan/350°F/gas 4.

Place 2 apricots or prunes into the centre of each pineapple ring – cover tightly with aluminium foil and cook for 50 minutes.

'ALL-IN-RED' BRAISED RED CABBAGE

SERVES 10–12

One September I harvested a marvellous crop of home-grown red cabbages. I pickled some, made coleslaw with one and made this delicious braised red cabbage which freezes well so would keep till Christmas. This can be cooked in a low-temperature conventional oven, or the simmering oven of the Aga or slow cooker. I call this my 'all-in-red' braised red cabbage because most of the ingredients are gorgeously red, warm and seasonal. Serve with roast turkey and duck – in fact, as a hot colourful vegetable at any meal.

25g butter
2 red onions, thinly sliced
1–1.5kg red cabbage,
    thinly sliced
2 garlic cloves,
    thinly sliced
Seeds of 1 pomegranate
    (see Tip)
3 tbsp cranberry sauce
    or raspberry jam
½ tsp ground mace or
    1 tsp ground nutmeg
½ tsp ground cinnamon
2–3 tbsp red wine, port
    or cranberry juice
2 tsp salt and
    1½ tsp pepper

You will need:
Chopping board
    and sharp knife
Digital weighing scales
Measuring spoons
Large ovenproof casserole
    dish with a well-fitting
    lid or slow cooker
Wooden spoon

Preheat the oven to 100°C/80°C fan/210°F/gas ¼ or use a slow cooker or the bottom (simmering) oven of an Aga.

Add the butter to the casserole dish and place over a medium heat. Add the sliced onions and fry for 5–10 minutes until softened, then add the sliced cabbage, garlic and pomegranate seeds followed by the rest of the ingredients. Give everything a really good stir. Cover, pop into the oven and braise slowly for 2–2½ hours, stirring halfway through. It is sufficiently cooked when the cabbage and onion are tender and everything is glossy and deep red in colour.

Remove from the oven and taste, adjusting the seasoning if necessary. You may want to add more salt or sweetness depending how you like it. If you want to freeze it, leave it to cool completely then pack into a plastic box or bags. When ready to use, thaw overnight in the fridge or in a pan in a cool place then reheat slowly – either in the original casserole dish in the oven at 120°C/100°C fan/250°F/gas ½ or a slow cooker until piping hot.

TIP
I cut the pomegranate in half over the pan to make sure I catch the juice, then turn each half inside out. Some seeds will pop out by themselves, while the others can be easily taken out by hand.

WINTER

CRANBERRY ROAST

SERVES 3–4 (OR 6–8 AS A SIDE DISH)

When the family gather round the table for Christmas dinner I have an extra roast on offer for the vegetarians amongst us, but I find others like a portion of this on the side too!

40g pine nuts
3 tbsp vegetable oil
1 large onion,
   finely chopped
1 garlic clove,
   finely chopped
1 tsp dried mixed herbs
1 celery stick,
   finely chopped
1 medium carrot,
   finely chopped
8 juniper berries,
   crushed, or 1 tbsp
   fresh chopped rosemary
250g chestnut
   mushrooms,
   thinly sliced
1 tsp ground nutmeg
4 tbsp chopped
   fresh parsley
400g tin of chickpeas,
   drained and rinsed
1 large egg
2 tbsp Dijon mustard
2 tbsp HP sauce, tomato
   ketchup (or home-
   made, page 238)
Butter, for greasing
   and frying
2 tbsp grated cheese
100g coarse fresh
   breadcrumbs
3 tbsp cranberry sauce
Salt and pepper

Heat the frying pan (which will be used to prep all of the ingredients for this roast) and dry roast the pine nuts. Keep a close eye on them as they can soon burn. Keep the pan moving, and once golden in colour, transfer them to the large mixing bowl.

Heat the vegetable oil in the same pan and fry the onion until just starting to soften and colour. Add the garlic and dried herbs followed by the celery, carrot, juniper berries or rosemary, salt and pepper. Allow to cook for 5 minutes then transfer to the bowl with the pine nuts.

Heat another tablespoon of oil in the pan then add the mushrooms and nutmeg. Keep stirring until the mushrooms brown well. Transfer these to the bowl with all the other ingredients. Add the parsley directly to the bowl and give everything a good mix. Have a taste at this stage and add more seasoning if required.

Place the chickpeas in the bowl of a food processor and blitz to a rough paste. If you don't have a processor, mash the chickpeas in a bowl with a potato masher to a thick puree. Add the egg, mustard and HP sauce or ketchup and blitz again (or mix with a fork) until you have a smooth puree. Add the ingredients from the bowl and allow the mixer to blitz for a second or two – you want a mixture that is well combined but still has some structure to it. If making by hand, simply thoroughly mix the puree into the bowl of vegetables.

Transfer the mixture to the ovenproof dish greased with butter, smooth out, then sprinkle over the grated cheese.

You will need:
Large frying pan
Large mixing bowl
Chopping board
Knife
Measuring spoons
Wooden spoon
Food processor
    or potato masher
Ovenproof dish lightly
    greased – mine
    measures 23 x 16 x 6cm
    (9 x 6 x 2¼ inches)
Grater

Back to the frying pan. Heat another tablespoon of oil and a knob of butter until the butter melts and begins to froth, then pop in the breadcrumbs and stir well, allowing them to become coated in the fats. Turn down the heat and add the cranberry sauce. The sauce will begin to dissolve amongst the breadcrumbs. Remove the pan from the heat and transfer to the dish with the rest of the ingredients. Spread over the breadcrumbs so that they cover the whole of the roast. The dish can now be chilled or frozen and cooked when needed.

Preheat the oven to 190°C/170°C fan/375°F/gas 5 and cook the cranberry roast for about 30 minutes (45 minutes from frozen) or until the top is crunchy and golden and the inside is bubbling.

Serve in squares with lashings of gravy – vegetarian, of course (see page 208) – and all the Christmas veg.

ALL-IN-ONE CRANBERRY SAUCE

MAKES 2 300G JARS (OR GIVE SMALL JARS AS GIFTS)

If you buy your cranberry sauce because making your own seems just one step too far at Christmas then let me persuade you to try this. So easy – in fact it makes itself.

When I examined a jar of store-bought sauce and saw that it contained only 30% cranberries – the rest being mostly sugar and water – I worked on my own recipe which boasts 76% fruit, so don't buy it! This recipe is for the hob but you could easily adapt it for the oven, slow cooker, microwave or multi-cooker.

300g fresh cranberries
Zest and juice of
    1 large orange
120g sugar
2 tbsp of your favourite
    tipple (optional) –
    Cointreau works well

You will need:
Zester
Saucepan and lid
2 x 300g jars with lids

Add the ingredients to the saucepan, stir well then cover with a lid. Bring to a slow simmer (not a high heat because the base of your pan can burn) on the hob and stir from time to time until the cranberries soften.

The sauce is cooked through when the cranberries can easily be squashed with a fork. Leave to cool completely. Can be stored in clean sterilised jars (see page 231) or in the fridge for at least six weeks. It freezes well.

BALSAMIC-GLAZED SLOW-ROAST BRISKET OF BEEF WITH YORKSHIRE PUDDINGS

SERVES 6-8

Whenever I hear the word 'brisket' I am forced to smile. Many years ago, when I was easily influenced, I remember a work colleague telling me she had enjoyed roast beef for Sunday lunch the day before. My response was, 'Was it brisket?', as that was the only cut of meat I knew. 'Oh no,' she said. 'That's what poor people eat!' Fast-forward forty years or so and we see brisket served up in the very best establishments – my sister-in-law telling me she saw it on the menu at The Ritz!

You will not be disappointed with the flavours of this economical cut of beef. Choose a lean piece of rolled brisket of beef from your butcher. Served with Yorkshire puddings (page 191) and all the Sunday trimmings, your roast beef per head will be a quarter of the price of a top-end cut.

2.5kg lean rolled
    brisket of beef
Freshly ground
    black pepper
4 garlic cloves, unpeeled
300ml hot beef or
    chicken stock

For the gravy:
Juices from the
    roasting pan
2–3 tsp plain flour,
    cornflour or
    gravy browning

For the balsamic glaze:
50ml balsamic vinegar
3 tsp sugar

You will need:
Kitchen paper
Roasting tin and
    foil to cover tightly,
    or slow cooker
Digital weighing scales
Sieve
Mug

Preheat the oven to 100°C/80°C fan/210°F/gas ¼ or use the bottom (simmering) oven of the Aga.

Start by drying off the meat with kitchen paper then sprinkle it generously with black pepper. Place the garlic in the bottom of the tin or slow cooker then pop the meat on top. Add the hot stock then cover with a tent of foil so that air can circulate inside (don't put the foil on so tight that it hugs the meat closely). If putting in a slow cooker put a layer of foil over the pot before putting the lid on, that way everything is airtight.

Slow-roast for 12 hours – I put mine in the oven at 8.30pm and took it out at 8.30am the next morning. Carefully remove the foil then put your meat on a plate and leave it to go completely cold – do not put it in the fridge.

You will be left with a pool of delicious juices that can be strained through a sieve then chilled in the fridge. A layer of fat may form on the top, so remove this if you prefer, then thicken your stock with flour, cornflour or your favourite gravy browning, or even add a tablespoon of fresh breadcrumbs to stir through and thicken. (I actually prefer my gravy with the fat, squashed garlic cloves and cooking juices, but if you want a really smooth gravy, follow the instructions above.)

Recipe continued overleaf

Wooden spoon
Small saucepan
Kitchen scissors
Serrated knife
Pastry brush

TIP
If you want to roast a smaller piece of beef then choose a piece weighing around 1kg and cook for 8 hours using half the stock and garlic.

I usually take a kitchen mug, add 2–3 teaspoons of flour or cornflour and a teaspoon of gravy browning then a little cold water and stir with a teaspoon to make a paste. Add more cold water so that the mug resembles a cup of cold coffee then pour this over the meat juices and stock in the pan. Bring to the boil and stir all the time until the gravy thickens. Too thick – add more water; too thin – mix another simple paste in your mug.

The gravy can be made ahead and reheated – I freeze leftover gravy if there is any, it always comes in handy.

To make the balsamic glaze, put the balsamic vinegar in a small pan with the sugar and boil until it reduces down to the thickness of syrup – about 5 minutes. Allow to cool.

When ready to serve, remove the string from the cold meat. Slice the meat thinly – it is much easier to do when it is cold as the meat will be quite firm. Place the slices of meat in a small roasting tin lined with foil then paint over your balsamic glaze.

Preheat the oven to 200°C/180°C fan/400°F/gas 6, then cook your meat for 20 minutes until it is heated through and the glaze is dark and shiny. Keep warm while the Yorkshire puddings cook.

YORKSHIRE PUDDINGS

MAKES 12

Being a Yorkshire lass, I am often asked how to make a good Yorkshire pud! A good pudding is light and very well risen with a crisp yet soft texture, and not hard, rubbery or doughy.

A traditional Yorkshire pudding is about 7.5cm (3 inches) wide and about 5cm (2 inches) tall and would have been served with gravy before the main course of roast beef. Any leftovers would have been eaten with golden syrup, jam or lemon curd.

Nowadays we tend to serve smaller Yorkshire puddings with the main course. A 12-hole muffin tin is perfect and this recipe will give you 12 beautifully risen, light, golden puddings.

140g plain flour
5g salt
1 tsp ground white pepper
4 large eggs
140ml whole milk
60ml cold water
20g beef dripping

You will need:
Measuring jug
Digital weighing scales
Large mixing bowl
Fork
12-hole deep muffin tin

TIP
For a really smooth batter I always mix by hand just using a fork. My Yorkshire pudding tin is well seasoned. I never wash it! It is a tin, blackened over time, that is used for nothing other than my perfect puddings.

TIP
You can transfer the batter to a large jug and keep in the fridge till you are ready for it – if it has separated just add another 20ml water and beat with a fork.

In a large mixing bowl put the flour, salt and pepper. Make a well in the centre then add an egg. Use a fork to mix the egg with a little of the flour, still maintaining the well in the centre. Add the rest of the eggs one by one and continue to mix to a very thick mixture, bringing the flour into the well little by little. Eventually you will achieve a really thick mix – even thicker than a cake mix. Keep beating with the fork until you see that every lump of flour has been absorbed and you have a smooth yet thick dough. Now you can begin to add your liquids. Start a little at a time with the milk and once the milk has been incorporated add the water. Mixing is now easier, the batter will be the consistency of thick unwhipped cream and there will be no lumps.

Place a thumbnail-sized piece of fat into each hole of the tin. Pop the tin into the cold oven then turn it on and allow it to come to a temperature of 240°C/220°C fan/460°F/gas 7.

When the oven has come to temperature take the tin out. The fat and tin will be very hot! Pour the batter into each cup filling to about three-quarters full then pop it straight back into the oven. Bake for 25 minutes. After 15 minutes your puddings will be well risen and brown and you may feel they are ready but if you take them out this early they will sink. Turn the oven down to 180°C/160°C fan/350°F/gas 4 for the remaining cooking time.

Serve immediately. You can freeze any leftovers but they are not as delicious as those served fresh from the oven.

SAVOURY STUFFING CROWD-PLEASER

SERVES 12–16

Cooking for a crowd at Christmas and during holiday times needn't be over complicated, and I like to prepare as much food in advance as is possible. One of those dishes is the stuffing! Rather than tediously forming stuffing into balls, I now use my bundt tin to present a show-stopping savoury stuffing wreath – it really is a winner! Fresh sage leaves are plentiful and an all-year-round good provider in my garden.

20 fresh sage leaves,
 half roughly chopped
30g butter
2 onions, finely chopped
1 apple, diced (skin on)
1kg good-quality
 sausage meat
60g fresh breadcrumbs
Zest of 1 lemon
1 tbsp dried mixed herbs
Grinding of black pepper

You will need:
Metal bundt tin or baking
 tin, well greased or use
 Lining Paste (page 86)
Frying pan
Mixing bowl
Chopping board
 and knife
Zester
Wooden spoon

Brush the bundt tin with lining paste then arrange half of the fresh sage leaves (right-side down) of even sizes around the inside of the tin. The leaves will adhere nicely to the paste. Once turned out, the stuffing wreath will be proudly decorated.

Heat the butter in a frying pan and fry the onions for about 10 minutes until softened and just starting to colour. Take the pan off the heat then add the diced apple and stir around to coat with the butter and prevent it going brown. Leave to cool in the pan.

In the mixing bowl add the sausage meat. Add the remaining sage leaves to the bowl along with the breadcrumbs, lemon zest, dried mixed herbs and freshly ground pepper. Add the cooled onion and apple and mix together well. I tend to use my hands to mix – it's much easier.

Take handfuls of the mixed stuffing and drop them directly over a sage leaf in the tin so they are not disturbed from their placed positions. Once the bundt tin has been filled with stuffing, use your hands to gently even it out and smooth the top.

At this stage the stuffing can be frozen or cooked.

Preheat the oven to 200°C/180°C fan/400°F/gas 6, then cook for 50 minutes from frozen or 35 minutes from chilled. The stuffing will be cooked to golden brown then flipped out onto a warm serving plate and taken to the table as it is.

This is a big hit around our Christmas table!

RED CABBAGE COLESLAW

SERVES 8-10

This is the perfect winter salad and I adore this colourful accompaniment particularly with jacket potatoes. For a summer white cabbage coleslaw, make this using white cabbage, a bunch of spring onions, any other dried fruits, add chopped nuts and scatter over fresh parsley, coriander or basil when ready to serve.

1 red cabbage
1 carrot
1 red onion
100g dried cranberries

For the dressing:
150ml plain yoghurt
3 tsp English mustard
4 tbsp mayonnaise
1 tbsp malt vinegar
2 tbsp salad cream

You will need:
Chopping board
Sharp knife
Large bowl
Measuring spoons
Screw-top jar
Course grater or use
    a food processor

Either very thinly slice all the vegetables by hand or put the slicing blade on a food processor and slice – chop the cranberries too. Transfer all the vegetables and the cranberries into a very roomy bowl.

Put all the dressing ingredients into a screw-top jar and give them a good shake. Pour the dressing over the shredded vegetables, stir, cover and put into the fridge for several hours or overnight to allow the flavours to develop.

AN EASY TRIFLE SPONGE

MAKES 35 SQUARES

You can buy trifle sponges from the supermarket but they are one of those ultra-processed bakes that have a very long shelf life – months, in fact – so for the extra little bit of effort when the oven goes on for something else I make a batch of sponges that can be frozen for up to 4 months, for when I want to make this trifle – perfect for any celebration.
This little trifle sponge recipe can also easily be made gluten-free.

3 large eggs
75g caster sugar
75g plain flour
    (or gluten-free
    plain flour)

You will need:
Swiss roll tin
    or lipped baking
    tray 37 x 26 x 2cm
    (14 x 10 x ¾ inch),
    well greased or use
    Lining Paste (page 86)
Mixing bowl
Hand-held electric whisk
Sieve
Large metal spoon
Angled palette knife
    or teaspoon
Knife

The oven temperature needs to be 180°C/160°C fan/ 350°F/gas 4.

Crack the eggs into the mixing bowl and add the caster sugar. Whisk on high speed with the hand-held electric whisk for 5 minutes until the mixture has doubled in size, is paler in colour and the whisks when taken from the mix leave a trail on the surface. Sift over the flour then use the large metal spoon to slowly and carefully fold the flour into the light batter. This takes a few minutes to get it right – don't rush it, as you need to retain the air. You will regularly see unmixed flour appear in the batter. Mix slowly in large regular stirs and you will see that the batter has thickened, is smooth and no flour remains. Don't be tempted to reach for the electric whisk to speed things up.

Transfer the mixture into the prepared tin and use an angled palette knife or teaspoon to push the mixture into the corners of the tin. This batter will not flow and find its own level, so it is important that you smooth it out evenly and that it has an even thickness. Pay attention to the edges of the tin and make sure the level is the same at the edges as it is in the middle, to ensure even baking.

Bake for 8–10 minutes until slightly risen and pale golden. Take from the oven and leave to cool completely in the tin.

Once cold, cut the sponge into 35 x 5cm (2 inch) squares – or whatever sizes you prefer – then use what you need in the trifle overleaf and freeze the rest.

SIMPLE SHERRY TRIFLE

SERVES 6–8

This very simple trifle goes onto the menu every Christmas and has done for many decades. It tastes great, even though there are no frills, nothing fancy and no special ingredients.

For the jelly layer:
6–8 trifle sponge pieces
    (see page 197)
100g frozen raspberries
    or mixed soft berries
6 tbsp sherry (optional)
135g packet jelly (I use
    raspberry, strawberry
    or cherry)

For the custard layer
4 tbsp Bird's custard
    powder or use 4 tbsp
    cornflour, ½ tsp Vanilla
    Extract (page 213) and
    a drop of natural yellow
    food colouring
3 tbsp sugar
500ml milk

For the cream layer
300ml double cream
2 tsp icing sugar
2 tbsp flaked almonds,
    sprinkles, silver balls
    or chocolate shards

You will need:
Deep glass serving dish
    around 3-litre capacity
2 x glass or plastic
    measuring jugs –
    1 x 500ml and 1 x 1 litre
Saucepan
Mixing bowl
Hand-held electric whisk
Measuring spoons

Lay the trifle sponges in the dish then scatter over the frozen berries. Add a tablespoon of sherry to each sponge and leave to soak in while you make the jelly.

Make the jelly according to the packet instructions. I tend to break the cubes into the bottom of a microwave-safe 500ml jug, add half a pint of cold water and microwave on High in 30-second bursts until the gelatine dissolves. Top up with cold water to almost 1 pint – less about 2–3 tablespoons as there is liquid from the berries and the sherry, so don't make up a full pint of jelly. Pour the liquid jelly over the fruit and sponges and transfer to the fridge to set. You can do this 1–2 days in advance.

Meanwhile, prepare the custard layer (this can also be done the day before, if you prefer). I use custard powder for my trifle – it is quick, easy, egg-free and gluten-free, and cheaper than making a traditional crème anglaise. Measure the custard powder into a microwave-safe 1-litre jug, add the sugar and 2–3 tablespoons of the milk, and mix to a thick, smooth paste. Then add the rest of the milk. Transfer to the microwave and cook on High in 1-minute bursts, stirring between each addition. The custard will thicken in 5–7 minutes. Alternatively, the custard mix can be heated in a pan on the hob slowly, stirring all the time until thickened.

Don't be tempted to pour this hot custard straight onto the jelly layer – the heat from the custard will start to dissolve the jelly and although it will reset when chilled there will not be a neat distinction between layers. Leave the custard to stand in the jug or the pan for 30 minutes or so, stirring from time to time to prevent a skin forming. Once cooled to warm rather than hot it can be poured over the set jelly. Pop the trifle back into the fridge so that the custard cools completely, forms a skin and sets.

TIP

Fruits will float to the top of the jelly, so if you want them to sit at the bottom of the bowl or have a more even distribution, cover a few fruits with a little jelly taken from the jug. Transfer to the fridge and allow this to set – this should take an hour. Leave the rest of the jelly out on the work surface at room temperature. Once the bottom layer of jelly has set then cover with the sponges, sherry and the rest of the fruits then pour over the rest of the jelly. If, while the remaining jelly in the jug has been standing it has thickened or set, just 10 seconds in the microwave will loosen it again. Don't allow it to boil.

TIP

If you want to make your own jelly, use 1 gelatine leaf per 100ml fruit juice or use Vege-Gel according to the packet instructions.

On the day of serving, whisk the double cream and icing sugar together in a mixing bowl with a hand-held electric whisk until very soft (almost sloppy) peaks. Be careful not to over-whisk (see Tip). Spoon loosely over the set custard and decorate with toasted almonds, sprinkles or silver chocolate balls or simple chocolate shards.

Serve chilled.

TIP

If you do over-whip your double cream and it has gone from being smooth and light to crumbly, stiff and resembling cottage cheese, it can be rescued. Remove the whisks, scraping off as much over-whipped cream as is possible with a knife. Use a hand whisk (not electric) to slowly stir in a little milk or cream – one or two tablespoons at a time. Stir slowly at first to loosen the thickened cream and mix the liquid into it. The two will emulsify, just keep adding milk or cream until you can freely whisk the cream, it is smooth and silky once more and can be used.

VARIATION: VEGAN TRIFLE

It's easy to make this trifle vegan with a few simple swaps.

Make up the jelly layer using Vege-Gel – follow the packet instructions to set 500ml (1 pint) of jelly, or you can use any fruit juice to set.

Use frozen berries as for the standard trifle, but omit the sponges and alcohol.

For the custard layer, follow the instructions and use non-dairy milk.

For the cream layer, chill a tin of full-fat coconut cream in the fridge overnight. Use only the solids and whip up with 1–2 teaspoons of sugar, or use a plant-based double cream.

MAKE IT YOURSELF!

In this chapter I have taken a number of everyday store-cupboard items
to give you some ideas for making your own – not only to save money
but to be able to understand and control what is being consumed.
I spend more and more time examining the reverse labels on foods
in the supermarket to help me decide which ingredients I want
to avoid, change up or leave out of my diet altogether.

INSTANT VEGGIE STOCK CUBES

MAKES 25–30 (15–20G) INSTANT STOCK CUBES

When it comes to a full-flavoured soup, stew, casserole, savoury pie or gravy, a good stock is essential. You may be really organised and make your own stock, which is fantastic, but there are those occasions when an instant stock cube dissolved in boiling water does the job quickly and easily. I had a field day when it came to examination of the reverse labels – I didn't expect to see palm oil and there were a significant number of unexplained other ingredients in the form of colours, flavours and preservatives that I could neither spell nor pronounce. I then calculated that the 10g stock cubes in my pantry were between 25% and 40% salt. So I decided to make my own, and these are a really useful and flavoursome low-salt version.

1–2 tbsp oil
2 carrots, very
    finely chopped
1 leek, washed and
    very finely chopped
1 celery stick, very
    finely chopped
1 small potato, very finely
    chopped (optional)
1 onion, very
    finely chopped
3 garlic cloves, very
    finely chopped
Bunch of fresh herbs
    (parsley, 2 bay leaves,
    sage, rosemary)
1 tbsp mixed dried herbs
½ tsp ground cumin
1 tsp ground turmeric
1 tsp ground black pepper
25–40g sea salt flakes, or
    leave salt out altogether
20g cornflour or potato
    starch (optional)

You will need:
Large frying pan or
    casserole dish with lid
Chopping board
Knife
Stick blender, liquidiser
    or potato masher
Ice-cube trays

Heat the oil in the large frying pan or casserole dish over a high heat, then add the chopped vegetables, fresh and dried herbs, spices and seasoning and fry for 5 minutes, stirring to prevent burning. Turn the heat down to its lowest, cover with the lid and cook very gently for 20 minutes or until the vegetables are soft. Lift the lid and stir from time to time. Transfer to a large bowl and remove any stalks from the fresh herbs, plus the bay leaves.

Add the cornflour or potato starch to the hot veggies, if using, and stir well (omit if a potato was used with the veggies). Using the stick blender, liquidiser or potato masher, blitz, blend or mash to a very thick puree. Allow to cool and thicken further.

Pipe or spoon the puree into ice-cube trays or silicone moulds and freeze. Once frozen, remove from the trays and store in a box in the freezer.

To make an instant full-flavoured stock, add a 15–20g cube to a heatproof jug and pour over 500ml boiling water. Stir until the cube dissolves and you're good to go.

GRAVY

SERVES 4

Making a tasty gravy from scratch with no stock or meat juices can be a challenge, and maybe that's why there are so many 'instant' gravy solutions on the market. However, instant gravy granules can needlessly add too much salt to your diet. I did a bit of research and found that for every 100g of gravy granules, 24g was salt. Not great if you are watching your blood pressure.

Here is a recipe that is very good indeed for several reasons: you know exactly what is going into it, it can be adapted to suit gluten-free, low-salt, vegan and dairy-free diets, and, most importantly, it tastes great. If you are serving sausages or toad in the hole, make this gravy. If you are serving a meat pie, try substituting the apple juice for stout or simply stick with the stock option. The apple juice can also be substituted with cider for pork and sausages. Either way, it's a good standby recipe. This gravy will freeze well so try batch cooking to then freeze in handy portions.

2 tbsp oil
Knob of butter
2 medium onions,
    very finely chopped
1½ tbsp dried mixed herbs
2 garlic cloves, finely
    chopped, or use
    ½ tsp garlic powder
2 tbsp Dijon or
    English mustard
2 tbsp browned flour
    (see Tip)
300ml vegetable stock
    (see page 206), chicken
    stock (see page 140),
    apple juice, cider
    or stout
Pinch of salt and
    ½ tsp freshly ground
    black pepper

You will need:
Large frying pan
    or casserole
Chopping board
    and knife
Measuring spoons
Digital weighing scales
Jug
Wooden spoon or spatula
Stick blender

In a frying pan over a low–medium heat, heat the oil and butter then add the onions and dried mixed herbs and fry until the onions are well browned. Don't rush this – the onions will probably take about 20 minutes to cook well, becoming soft and dark golden in colour.

Add the chopped or powdered garlic and cook for a further 2–3 minutes. Then add the mustard and flour and stir this into the onions. Cook for about a minute, then little by little add the stock or equivalent and 200ml water, stirring well to avoid any lumps. Turn up the heat and the gravy will start to thicken. Taste and check the seasoning. Stir well and allow to cook for a few minutes.

The gravy can be served as it is but if you prefer a smooth gravy, blitz with a stick blender.

TIP
Just as toasting seeds, nuts and spices brings out their flavour, the same applies to flour. Cover a lipped baking tray with a sheet of reusable baking parchment then sprinkle over flour to cover. When the oven goes on for something else, brown some flour. As an experiment, dip a finger in the flour and taste before toasting – pretty tasteless, I'd say. Brown in the oven until the flour is pale caramel in colour, take from the oven and taste again – yummy! Allow to cool on the tray then transfer to a jar to keep for thickening soups, stews, gravy, sauces, etc.

VANILLA EXTRACT

MAKES 70ML

Vanilla pods are very expensive, and for that reason I have in the past relied on cheaper extracts and pastes, but even these can vary in price enormously depending on quality. At the lower end of the scale is the much more affordable vanilla essence – costing around a tenth of the price of the best vanilla extract. The best-quality vanilla extract is obviously the most expensive and some of the cheaper ones lack depth of flavour, meaning more is needed and therefore it isn't as cheap as it seems.

I delved into the ingredients lists of some extracts to discover that the percentage of real vanilla can vary enormously. More worrying for me was discovering that the affordable 'vanilla essence' I had used many a time had never even seen a vanilla pod or seeds and had been concocted in a laboratory using a cocktail of synthetic chemicals, flavourings and colourings.

However, it is easy to make at home – just two or three ingredients and 8 weeks of patience, and you'll never run out!

1 organic vanilla pod
70ml vodka (or brandy, whisky or rum) or 60ml vegetable glycerine and 10ml bottled water

You will need:
Chopping board
Small sharp pointed knife
Kitchen scissors
Small 100ml glass jar or bottle (washed and sterilised, page 231) with a well-fitting lid or cap
Measuring jug
Small funnel
36ml reused vanilla extract or glycerine bottle

TIP
I use vodka for this so that I can see the change in colour of the liquid, but for a non-alcohol vanilla extract, snip the vanilla pod as before, place into the jar and add 60ml vegetable glycerine and 10ml bottled water.

Lay the vanilla pod onto a chopping board and, using a small, sharp pointed knife, slice down the pod lengthways, thereby opening it up to expose the seeds. Snip the two halves of the vanilla pod into small pieces about 1.25cm (½in) in length and pop into the clean glass jar or bottle.

Top up with the vodka or spirit of choice. Ensure there is some head space in the jar or bottle being used because the extract needs a good shake once a week.

Keep in a cool dark place (mine lives in my spice drawer), shake at least once a week and see the clear spirit slowly turn a gorgeous caramel colour as the vanilla infuses. Leave at least 8 weeks (the longer the better) – 3 months gave me the best result.

After 8 weeks or so 30ml of the home-made vanilla extract can be poured off into a previously used vanilla extract bottle and used in the same quantities and measures as directed in any recipe.

This vanilla extract is 'ongoing', because the jar containing the vanilla pod pieces can be topped up with either more vodka or vegetable glycerine. I use the pod pieces three or four times and my mix will keep for over a year.

EASY VANILLA ICE CREAM

MAKES 1 LITRE

When examining the list of ultra-processed foods in the supermarket, ice cream comes high on it. This recipe of mine, however, is super simple, tastes delicious and is inexpensive. If you have an ice-cream machine the results are smooth and luscious, but if not, here's how to get a very good result. I use evaporated milk, which can be considered a processed food product as it undergoes various steps such as heating, homogenisation and canning to produce the final product. But it is made from all-natural ingredients and does not contain any artificial preservatives or flavourings. Try serving the warm Brownie (on page 114), with warm Espresso Sauce (page 212) and a scoop of this home-made vanilla ice cream – a delicious dessert!

2 large eggs
50g caster sugar
1½ tsp Vanilla Extract
   (page 213) or if you
   want to make your ice
   cream really special –
   half a vanilla pod,
   seeds scraped
400ml tin of evaporated
   milk, chilled overnight
   in the fridge

You will need:
Small saucepan
2 mixing bowls – one
   heatproof and one
   placed in the fridge for
   at least an hour to chill
Hand-held electric whisk
Digital weighing scales
1litre plastic tub (reuse
   an old ice cream carton
   or roomy plastic bowl
   that has a lid)

Bring a small pan of water to the boil then turn off the heat. In the heatproof mixing bowl whisk the eggs, sugar and vanilla together. Place over the pan of hot recently-boiled water and whisk continually with the hand-held electric whisk until the mixture thickens, turns pale in colour and when the whisks are lifted out they leave a ribbon trail on the mixture. The eggs will be cooked and the mixture will have increased in volume. Take the bowl off the heat and set aside.

Take the chilled bowl from the fridge and pour into it the chilled evaporated milk. With the same whisks, whip up the evaporated milk until it too is thick and doubled in volume.

Stir the two mixes together then transfer to an ice-cream machine and churn until thick, smooth and iced – about 50 minutes – then either transfer to a 1-litre plastic tub and place in the freezer or eat at once! If you do not have an ice-cream machine, transfer your whipped-up mixture to a roomy plastic bowl which has a lid. Transfer to the freezer and leave for 1½ hours. Take from the freezer and whisk either by hand or with your electric whisk. This breaks down any ice particles that may be forming and incorporates some air into your mixture. Place back into the freezer. After another hour, repeat as above. Your ice cream should be setting and by giving this final whisk you will achieve a light, delicious (home-churned) vanilla ice cream.

If, when you take it from the freezer, it is frozen hard leave to soften in the fridge for about half an hour to an hour before serving. This ice cream is best eaten within 3 months.

SPRAY OIL

MAKES 1 BOTTLE

Oil sprays for cooking are very popular, as they promise a light spray of oil to coat pans before frying and to quickly grease baking tins. I use a spray of oil over my home-made fishcakes, fish fingers, chicken Kyivs and croquettes before air-frying or oven-baking.

As has become common practice nowadays, I critically examine what I am buying. I am promised a 'light and mild' spray cooking oil and then realise that is because it is diluted with water. In addition, I often spy a few extra unknown chemical additives, then of course there is the single-use plastic bottle thrown in for good measure. I now make my own. I have attempted to load a spray bottle with oil on its own but found the nozzle clogged and the spray just didn't work. By adding the water and vodka it worked a treat.

50ml oil of choice
  (I use olive oil)
50ml boiled and
  cooled water
½ tsp vodka (to help
  emulsify the oil
  and water)

You will need:
Plastic funnel
150ml glass spray bottle
  (plastic is fine, though
  glass easier to clean)
Measuring jug
Measuring spoons

For cleaning:
Plastic funnel
The oily 150ml bottle
2 tsp washing soda
3 drops eco-friendly
  washing-up liquid
2 tsp coarse salt flakes
2–3 tbsp hot water
  (plus more to fill)
Old toothbrush
1 tsp bicarbonate of soda

Place the funnel into the neck of the bottle then measure in first the oil then the water and vodka. Put the cap on, give it a shake and it is ready to use. Shake well before each use.

CLEANING

Oil is stubborn and difficult to clean from narrow-necked bottles – even my dishwasher doesn't manage it – so here is how to deep clean the glass bottle and spray attachment between refills:

Place the funnel into the neck of the bottle and add all of the cleaning ingredients. Screw on the cap and give it a really good shake – for several minutes. Remove the cap then fill the bottle to the neck with hot water. Replace the cap and leave for an hour or so. During this time the natural chemicals will do their job of breaking down the fat, the salt will dissolve and the whole lot can be safely poured down the sink.

A quick rinse and your oil spray bottle is as clean as a whistle and ready for a refill. To clean the nozzle, dip an old toothbrush in a little dry bicarbonate of soda to remove any oil residue, then rinse in warm water.

PASTA

We are so fond of pasta – I don't know anyone who says they don't like it, yet as a child growing up in the 1950s and 1960s pasta dishes were not commonplace.

Nowadays it is regularly on the menu at home, in restaurants, in supermarkets as both fresh and dried. It is considered a quick, easy and healthy meal. Children adore it, and as they love it so much I think they should know at an early age how to make it. I am not suggesting for one minute that we all make our pasta fresh from now on, but as an exercise to do with the kids or if you have half an hour spare, it is great and produces something far superior to anything bought in the supermarket!

My memory is taken back to one February school holiday when I was on childcare duties. I had four grandchildren for the day (ages ranging between 8 and 11) and rather than allowing them to become absolutely feral with excitement, my first job was to take them out in the cold wind and rain with the dogs for an hour's walk. They could splash in puddles and generally let off steam. When we got home I remember thinking that's one hour – only another seven to go!

Rather than plonk them in front of the TV or their devices I suggested instead that we make pasta. Their faces all aglow from the after-effects of the earlier weather beating, they formed a small hand-washing queue and we set to work.

There were no pots or bowls needed and therefore no washing up and it kept them quiet. I suggested there was a prize for the one that didn't breach their flour wall. That kept them focused, quiet and concentrating.

Little did they know at the outset that the prize for the winner was to be the first to turn the handle on the pasta maker!

FRESH PASTA

SERVES 2

Pasta can be made by machine using a dough hook but I prefer to get the radio on and knead it by hand. I do use a table-top pasta rolling machine – not essential but will give excellent results.

200g plain flour,
    pasta flour or '00' flour,
    plus extra for dusting
Pinch of salt
2 large eggs
Spray of oil (page 216)

You will need:
Digital weighing scales
Beeswax wrap or
    greaseproof paper,
    to cover
Pasta rolling machine
Rolling pin

TIP
A wooden spoon laid over the pan of boiling pasta will prevent it bubbling over.

To make the dough by hand, simply place the flour with the salt in a pile on a clean worktop, make a well in the centre and drop in the eggs. Using your index finger and middle finger from one hand, stir the eggs, bringing in the flour gradually until all of the flour has been incorporated. A challenge for the pasta maker is to keep the egg inside the walls of the flour and only gradually bring the dough together. One hand will be sticky and thick with dough but keep working and slowly after 10 minutes or so a ball of dough will form, the worktop will be clean and then you can easily knead by hand until the dough becomes smooth. I then like to rub both hands together to release any tiny dough bits that have stuck to the fingers, give my hands a spray of oil then finish kneading the pasta dough, gathering in any stray bits from the worktop.

With a little work your ball of pasta dough will be rich in colour, a little shiny and smooth. Wrap in a piece of greaseproof paper or a beeswax wrapper, then pop into the fridge for an hour to rest.

The best pasta is very thin and for that reason I recommend a pasta rolling machine, though a rolling pin can be used. Take half of the dough and shape into a small square, dust with flour then start to pass it through the machine, reducing the thickness every two turns. You will produce long, thick ribbons of pasta dough which can then be cut to size to make lasagne sheets, folded in half lengthways to make ravioli or cut into lengths then passed through the machine once more to cut spaghetti or tagliatelle. Alternatively, roll out as thinly as is possible using a rolling pin then cut out your preferred shapes using a steady hand and pizza cutter.

To cook, fill a large roomy saucepan three-quarters full with water, well salted, and bring to the boil. When you have a fast boil, drop in the pasta and cook for just 3 minutes. Strain through a colander then toss through with sauce.

BREAKFAST

Breakfast cereals are labelled as one of those everyday items that are mass produced and considered 'ultra-processed' because they often have extra ingredients added during production, such as emulsifiers, sweeteners and artificial colours and flavours. They are so very popular because they are convenient, kids love them and they come backed with lots of advertising and publicity – as well as excess sugar, salt and packaging!

When examining the reverse labels on certain 'quality' cereals I was still shocked at sugar and salt levels and other mystery ingredients, so I decided to make a few changes to my own diet and devise my own breakfast menu. It's still quick and convenient, but it's healthy!

I swap around between these breakfast recipes depending on the time of year.

MUESLI

MAKES 12–15 60G SERVINGS

If you have ever examined the ingredients on the back of your pack of muesli you may be astounded at the amount of additional sugar and salt included in some brands, and it can sometimes be bulked out with dried milk powder too.

My refined sugar- and salt-free version is now a staple in our house and once you've tried it there is no going back. The factory-produced versions cannot compare.

300g porridge oats
45g oat bran
½ tsp ground cinnamon
½ tsp nutmeg
45g toasted flaked
   almonds
70g pecan nuts or
   walnuts, chopped
150g mixed seeds
   (pumpkin, sunflower,
   poppy, chia, sesame
   and maybe goji
   berries for colour)
40g desiccated coconut
   or coconut flakes
100g ready-to-eat
   apricots

You will need:
Large mixing bowl
Spoon
1-litre glass jar or plastic
   storage container

Mix everything together in a large mixing bowl then transfer to the jar.

When serving, I use 60g per serving (about 4 tablespoons). Try soaking overnight in a little milk then top off with a blob of yoghurt and a few berries at breakfast. Yummy.

OVERNIGHT OATS (BIRCHER MUESLI)

SERVES 2

I was first introduced to overnight oats when I stayed in a hotel in London many years ago. It was a lovely hotel and the breakfast menu, well, I have to say it had everything you could imagine, from fried bacon and eggs to pancakes and porridge, to cheese and ham, fresh fruits and doughnuts then a vast selection of breads and pastries. It was a treasure trove.

Then I spotted Bircher muesli, which I had never heard of before and I just had to give it a go because it looked interesting. I adored this bowl for breakfast and wanted to know more about it.

So if you're also interested, Maximilian Bircher-Benner developed muesli in the early 1900s to help treat his patients (he was a Swiss doctor and nutritional pioneer). Using fresh fruits and oats he came up with a wholesome, tasty and easy-to-eat nutritious meal. It is now often referred to as overnight oats, and has many extra additions – and some include milk – but for me the delicious taste comes from the base which is oats simply soaked in apple juice the night before.

1 breakfast cup or
   mug of porridge oats
1 breakfast cup or
   mug of apple juice
1 tart apple (Granny
   Smith is a favourite)
1 tsp ground cinnamon
1 tbsp mixed seeds
1 tbsp mixed
   chopped nuts
2 tbsp plain full-fat
   yoghurt
1 tbsp honey or
   maple syrup
Blueberries, raspberries,
   strawberries or any
   fresh fruits

You will need:
Breakfast cup or mug
Mixing bowl
Plate
Measuring spoons
Sharp knife
Chopping board

The night before, place the oats in the bowl, pour over the apple juice, cover with a plate and pop into the fridge.

Next morning, wash the apple and finely dice – removing the core but leaving the skin on. Add this to the bowl along with the cinnamon, seeds and nuts. Stir through the yoghurt, honey or maple syrup and fresh fruits, and serve.

HOT (MICROWAVE) PORRIDGE

SERVES 2

Many people will have their own favourite porridge combo when a cold winter morning calls for something hot, wholesome and good for you; some like all milk with their oats – the Scots will have all water – I am a fan of half and half. I taught my kids to do porridge like this so that they could see to their own breakfast when necessary, and now my grandchildren do the same. Use non-dairy milk for a wholesome vegan breakfast.

Porridge oats
Milk (dairy or non-dairy)
Water

You will need:
1 breakfast mug
Medium microwave-safe
　glass bowl
Wooden or plastic
　spoon or spatula

The night before, fill the mug almost to the top with porridge oats and tip into a microwave-safe bowl. Use the same mug and fill to the same level with milk – that goes into the bowl, too. Finally, fill the mug to the same level with water and add to the bowl. Place the bowl in the fridge overnight.

Next morning, transfer the bowl to the microwave and cook on High for 3 minutes.

Stir with the wooden spoon or plastic spatula (which can be left in the bowl in the microwave as it's microwave-safe). Microwave for a further 1–2 minutes until the porridge is thickened and starting to boil. Stir, leave it to stand for 1 minute, then serve.

My family like either a sprinkling of demerara sugar, golden syrup, maple syrup or fruit with their porridge – I like it just as it is!

GRANOLA

MAKES 16–18 SERVINGS

I adore granola at breakfast, and while we consider it to be a healthy option – lots of fibre, nuts, seeds, oats, etc. – some brands can be deceptively high in fat and sugar. This recipe is easy and I have purposely kept the oil and sugar to a minimum. The toasting can be done in the oven or even in an air fryer!

300g porridge oats
½ tsp salt
1 tsp ground cinnamon
100g unsalted mixed nuts
  (such as walnuts, hazelnuts,
  cashews, almonds),
  roughly chopped
1 tbsp citrus crumb
  (optional) – made
  from blitzed-up dried
  orange peel (page 226)
100g mixed seeds (sesame,
  pumpkin, poppy, sunflower,
  flax seeds)
100g desiccated coconut
50ml honey or maple syrup
50ml oil of choice
  (I like olive oil)
150g ready-to-eat
  dried fruits (sultanas,
  cranberries, apricots,
  currants, raisins,
  prunes, figs)

You will need:
Digital weighing scales
Measuring spoons
Chopping board and knife
Large bowl
Large lipped baking tray
  lined with reusable
  baking parchment
Kitchen scissors
1-litre storage jar

Preheat the oven to 180°C/160°C fan/350°F/gas 4.

Add all the ingredients to the bowl apart from the dried fruits and give everything a good stir to mix. Spread out onto the lined baking tray and bake for 20 minutes, moving it all around halfway through. Alternatively, tip the ingredients into an air fryer for just 10 minutes, stirring regularly unless the air fryer has a paddle to keep the ingredients moving. This is sufficient to evenly toast the mix. Once tinged golden, remove from the oven and use the baking parchment as an aid to transfer everything back into the bowl.

Chop the dried fruits into even-sized pieces – leave raisins, cranberries and sultanas whole but use scissors to chop apricots, prunes and figs into smaller pieces.

Mix everything together and once cool transfer to the storage jar.

GRANOLA SUNDAY SUNDAE

SERVES 1

I like to make a yummy granola sundae for a perfect summer breakfast during the soft fruit season, as it feels quite a bit special and a weekend treat. This is made in minutes but will keep you going until lunch.

½ apple, cut into small dice,
   or 1 banana – or both
2 tbsp apple juice
A few blackberries
3 tbsp granola (page 225)
2–3 tbsp plain yoghurt
Raspberries, a few seeds
   and a sprinkle of orange
   crumb (see below)

You will need:
Chopping board and knife
Measuring spoons
1 glass serving bowl

Place the apple and/or banana into the bottom of the serving bowl and pour over the apple juice. Add the blackberries, followed by the granola then the yoghurt and decorate with raspberries, a few seeds and a sprinkle of citrus crumb.

CITRUS CRUMB

MAKES 1 450G (1 LB) JAR

Citrus fruit skins can be dried in the sun until crisp then blitzed to make the most gorgeous citrus crumb. The skin from one large grapefruit and two oranges fill a 450g glass jar and 1 tbsp crumb is equivalent to the fresh zest from one fruit. Free food and no waste!

Skin from assorted citrus
   fruits, e.g. 1 large
   grapefruit and
   2 oranges, washed

You will need:
Peeler
Sharp knife
Chopping board
Cooling rack
Liquidiser or food processor
Clean glass jar with a lid

Slice the peels into strips about 2.5cm (1 inch) thick – don't worry about the pith, it is edible and dries to such a thin layer that the bitterness is lost. Once blitzed, you will not detect it.

Lay the cut pieces onto a cooling rack and leave out in the sun or a warm room. The peels are sufficiently dried when they snap easily. The peels can also be dried in a low conventional oven or dehydrator.

Blitz the dried peels to a fine crumb in a sturdy liquidiser or food processor then store in a glass jar with a lid. The citrus blast given off when the lid is removed is wonderful.

YOGHURT

MAKES 3 500G JARS

I remember a time when the yoghurt market didn't exist in the UK, it was not something I had tasted as a child. Then in 1963, and about the time I started senior school, this new food became a fast-growing trend. The Swiss-invented Ski yoghurt had everyone buzzing, and to be 'up with the kids' it was really cool to take a pot to school. Yoghurt, sweetened and with added fruit – this was amazing. From then on yoghurt started a revolution on supermarket shelves.

Half a century later and we still enjoy yoghurt in its various forms but are discovering that some may not have the health benefits that maybe we expect. Added sugars or artificial sweeteners, synthetic flavours and colourings and maybe not as much real fruit could mean our daily yoghurt is not the nutritious breakfast we once thought.

There are yoghurt makers available to buy but yoghurt can also be easily made at home. The cost is half that of shop-bought, even after buying the best whole milk. It needs only two ingredients and a warm ambient temperature. An added advantage is no single-use plastic supermarket pot! This is a base recipe that can be adjusted to make as much or as little as you and your family will eat.

1 litre whole milk
3 heaped tsp thick
    full-fat natural yoghurt
    (for the first-ever batch)

You will need:
Saucepan
Large jug
Cooking thermometer
    (optional)
Tea towel
Plate to cover
3 x 500ml glass jars
Kettle of hot water
Spoon

Pour the milk into the saucepan and bring to the boil. Remove from the heat and pour into the jug, then set aside to cool. Boiling the milk will kill competing bacteria, allowing the whey proteins to coagulate and thicken and in time turn the milk into yoghurt.

The milk needs to cool down to a temperature of between 40 and 42°C (104 and 108°F). If you don't have a thermometer to check, the temperature feels like a warm 'hand-washing' heat – certainly not scalding and not as cool as tepid. Cover the jug of hot milk with a clean tea towel or cloth and a plate to prevent a skin forming.

While the milk is cooling, prepare the glass jars. Wash in warm soapy water, rinse, then fill each one with hot water from the kettle. This will keep the jars warm.

Once the milk has cooled sufficiently – mine took about 20 minutes – discard the water from the jars which should now feel just comfortably warm. Add a heaped teaspoon of plain full-fat yoghurt to the bottom of each jar and then divide the warm milk between them. No need to stir, simply seal the jars then leave in a warm place for 10 hours.

I tried a number of options and they all work well although my favourite is the dough proving setting of the oven because I can fit in 6 jars at a time.

- Wrap the jars in warm tea towels and stand on a barely warm radiator – if the mix gets too hot the yoghurt will not thicken.

- Stand the jars in an insulated bag and leave in a warm room.

- If your oven has a dough proving setting, this is the perfect temperature. Pop the jars into this very low oven for 10 hours.

- Preheat a slow cooker on low for 1 hour then add the jars and slow-cook for 2 hours, then switch off and leave the jars inside for 10 hours in total.

- Use a food thermos flask (one with a wide neck), first heated with boiling water before adding the warm milk.

After 10 hours check the yoghurt to make sure it has set. Transfer to the fridge, no need to stir.

Once made your home-made yoghurt will keep well and probably longer than shop-bought. I made a batch but then found myself with one unused jar and I was about to go on holiday. Should I discard it, bake with it or alternatively decide to put it to the test? A great opportunity to experiment!

I decided to leave it in the fridge while I was away.

The yoghurt, already over a week old, was absolutely fine when I returned home two weeks later.

PICKLING & PRESERVING

With any preserve, the vessel being used must be thoroughly clean and sterilised in order for the food inside to be well preserved. Don't assume you can skip this step. I remember once buying three brand-new jam jars to add to my recycled collection. I considered that because they were brand new and hadn't been used before that all they needed was a quick rinse. I filled my jars of jam only to find the three that I hadn't sterilised went mouldy, my reused and sterilised jars filled with the same jam were absolutely fine. Lesson learned.

I have two sterilising methods, one that uses the microwave, another the oven. After washing jars in hot soapy water, rinse then leave just a tablespoon of water in the base of each jar and pop them into the microwave. Sterilise as many jars as will fit onto the microwave turntable – usually up to 8 – then microwave on High for 60 seconds or until you see that the water in the base of each jar is bubbling away, then remove from the microwave. If only one or two jars are being sterilised, the microwave time can be reduced to around 15 seconds. Discard any remaining water then fill the hot jars with hot jams, pickles or preserves as per your recipe.

To sterilise metal lids, pop them into a small saucepan, cover with water, then bring to a boil and simmer for 10 minutes to sterilise. Do not re-use lids that have become rusted or where the rubber seal has perished. Replacement lids can be purchased for some jars.

If you don't have a microwave the jars can be sterilised in a conventional oven. Place clean jars in a cold oven, turn on to 100°C/80°C fan/210°F/gas ¼ for 30 minutes. Turn off the oven, leave the jars in there to keep warm until required. For Aga owners, clean jars can be placed in the bottom (simmering) oven for 30 minutes.

FRIDGE-PICKLED CUCUMBERS & ONIONS

SERVES 6-8

Made in minutes, this pickle is semi-sweet, the onions have been stripped of their 'rawness' and can be eaten without the unpleasant and long-lasting aftertaste and the mustard seeds and/or fresh chilli add interest, colour and a hint of spice! The cucumbers are still crisp and crunchy and it really is a delicious accompaniment to so many salads and meals, such as warm croquettes, or added to sandwiches, wraps, salads and more.

200ml white vinegar
50g sugar
¼ tsp salt
1 cucumber, thinly sliced
¼ red onion, thinly sliced
1 tsp mustard seeds
    (optional)
A few flecks of fresh
    chilli (optional)
Mint leaves or
    coriander leaves,
    to serve (optional)

You will need:
Measuring jug
Measuring spoons
Screw-top jar
Chopping board
    and knife
Mixing jug
Mixing bowl
Serving dish

Measure the vinegar, sugar and salt into the jar and shake well until the sugar and salt dissolve.

Add the cucumber, onion, mustard seeds or fresh chilli, if desired, to the mixing bowl. Pour over the sweetened vinegar, cover and place the bowl in the fridge for 1 hour.

Tip the pickles into a serving dish and scatter over a few fresh mint or coriander leaves to serve, if you like.

PICKLED RED CABBAGE

MAKES 6 450G (1 LB) JARS

This recipe is simple and delicious.

1kg red cabbage
   (before trimming)
50g salt
3 tbsp pickling spice
570ml malt vinegar
400g light brown sugar

You will need:
Digital weighing scales
Chopping board
   and knife
Colander
2 plates and weight
Measuring jug
Measuring spoons
Frying pan
Large saucepan with lid
Wooden spoon
Strainer
Large jug
6 glass jars with
   lids, sterilised
Teaspoon

TIP
Don't discard any surplus
spiced vinegar, transfer
to a vinegar bottle and
enjoy over chips or use
in cooking where any
recipe asks for vinegar.

Start the night before. Remove the outer leaves from the cabbage then cut in half and then into quarters. Remove the white core then shred very thinly. I tend to do this by hand – using a machine will inevitably produce a few large chunks rather than fine slices. Pile all of the shredded cabbage into the colander, sprinkle over the salt, put a plate over the top and weigh it down (I find a tin of beans works well) and a plate underneath to catch any juices. Leave overnight.

Sprinkle the pickling spice into a frying pan and dry-fry over a medium heat for just a few minutes. The heating and toasting will release the fragrant aroma of the spices. Remove any dried peppers or bay leaves in the mix as they will burn.

Transfer the toasted spices, plus any bay leaves and peppers into the large saucepan then pour over the vinegar and add the sugar. Place over a gentle heat and stir until the sugar dissolves. Bring the mixture to the boil then take from the heat, cover and leave in a cool place overnight so that the spices infuse the vinegar.

The next day, strain the spices from the vinegar by pouring the vinegar from the saucepan through a strainer and into a jug. Remove the plate from the cabbage, discard the juices that have drained onto the plate below. There is no need to rinse the cabbage. Pack the softened cabbage shreds tightly into the sterilised jars, leaving only about 1.25cm (½ inch) of space at the top. I find it easier to do this by hand then push down using the back of a teaspoon.

Pour over the spiced and sweetened vinegar, then seal and leave in a cool place away from direct sunlight for 2 months. Enough time for the cabbage to sweeten and soften – just perfect for Christmas.

Recipe continued overleaf

The recipe and method given for red cabbage can be used for so many vegetables. The overnight sprinkle of salt helps to sweeten and soften vegetables then the spiced vinegar can be used to pour over.

For example:

Pickled onions – you may want to leave the pickling spice in the jars rather than draining it out. My grandma used to, and they do look attractive in the jar amongst the onions.

Pickled beans (French beans and runner beans) – maybe use distilled white vinegar instead of brown malt vinegar to show off the green loveliness.

Pickled beetroot – cook the beetroot first then peel and slice. No need to cover with salt in the colander overnight.

Pickled peppers – try a milder pickling vinegar, using 1–2 tbsp mustard seeds rather than pickling spice and distilled white vinegar rather than malt.

MINT SAUCE

Delicious with so many dishes – in fact, my grandson enjoys it with everything! Rather than going out to buy a jar, you can make it yourself. Mint will grow anywhere during the summer, and this method will keep fresh mint preserved in vinegar until you are ready to make into a sauce to serve with your food.

A couple of large
  handfuls of mint leaves
1 tsp sugar per jar
200ml white wine
  vinegar or distilled
  white vinegar

You will need:
2–3 small (100ml) jars
  with lids
Chopping board and
  knife or food processor
Teaspoon
Measuring jug

Sterilise the jars (page 231). Chop the mint leaves very small – either do this by hand or in the small bowl of a food processor with the blade attached.

Transfer the chopped leaves into the jars, packing them quite tight, then pour over vinegar to cover. Add the sugar to each jar, screw on the top and store in a cool place.

When you want to use your mint sauce, take 1 teaspoon of the sauce and add 2–3 teaspoons of white wine vinegar, distilled white vinegar or lemon juice and serve.

MINT SALAD

SERVES 2–4

As well as serving with lamb and sausages, I like to make this salad to serve with curries.

½ cucumber, cut
  into dice (skin on)
100g cherry tomatoes,
  cut in half
1–2 spring onions,
  chopped small
  (or use 1 small onion)
Handful of radishes,
  sliced
1 tsp Mint Sauce
  (see above) and
  2–3 tsp lemon juice
1 tsp salt flakes
A few coriander leaves

Place all the chopped ingredients into a bowl or serving dish. Add the mint sauce and lemon juice, stir well, then sprinkle over the salt and fresh coriander leaves.

FRUIT KETCHUP

MAKES JUST OVER 1 LITRE

I think most homes probably have a bottle of brown sauce or ketchup on the shelf. Unfortunately, many often include artificial dyes, preservatives and flavours, which escalates them into the realm of ultra-processed foods. I have made this ketchup (a cross between tomato ketchup and brown sauce) for so many years, adjusting the fruits to suit whatever grows well that year.

Summer brings an abundance of fruit and I have developed this delicious recipe for a ketchup that will keep for at least a year. It takes a few hours but is well worth the effort. It is a firm favourite with adults and children in our family – with sausages, burgers, pork pie and cold meats. This makes just over 1 litre; you will need four or five glass bottles for storing it.

2kg plums, damsons
  and blackberries
  (I used 200g
  blackberries, 500g
  damsons – the rest
  were plums), stoned
250g onions,
  finely chopped
120g raisins
650ml malt vinegar
  (or try 300ml malt,
  300ml distilled
  white and 50ml
  balsamic vinegar)
25g sea salt crystals
1 tsp dried chilli flakes
1 tbsp black peppercorns
1 tbsp mustard seeds
Thumb-sized piece
  of fresh ginger,
  finely chopped
2 garlic cloves, sliced
1 star anise
4 whole cloves
225g brown sugar

Start by taking a very large pan and place the fruits into the pan. If the damsons are very small I don't bother to stone them as the stones will leave the fruits as they cook. Add the onions, along with the raisins and all other ingredients apart from the sugar.

Pop the pan over a medium heat, bring to the boil then turn the heat down to simmer for 30 minutes until the fruit is cooked and the onion is softened.

Stand the colander over the second pan. Pour the fruit pulp into the colander and use the wooden spoon to work the sauce through it and into the second pan.

I then like to strain the resulting thick puree a second time to remove any chilli flakes, mustard seeds, etc., so I pass it through a metal sieve back into the first pan. Discard and compost what's left in the metal sieve.

The very smooth puree is now ready for the sugar. Add the measured amount of sugar and stir over a medium heat until dissolved, then turn the heat down to a low simmer and allow the ketchup to reduce down to 1 litre or just over. This will give the ketchup exactly the right pouring consistency once bottled and cold. It usually takes about an hour – sometimes a bit longer, sometimes less time – it really depends on how ripe the fruits were.

You will need:
Chopping board
    and knife
2 large pans or
    casserole dishes
1 litre measuring jug
Colander
Wooden spoon
Metal sieve or strainer
Glass storage bottles
    with lids

TIP
Sauce bottles can be
purchased but I like to
save and reuse glass sauce
bottles. Give them a good
wash in warm soapy
water, rinse then place
in a cold oven. Switch
the oven on to 100°C/
80°C fan/210°F/gas ¼
and leave the bottles in
there to sterilise until
you are ready to fill them.
See tip on page 231 for
quick sterilising.

I tend to have a heatproof measuring jug alongside the pan
and after 45 minutes I pour the pan contents into the jug –
if I'm still well over 1 litre, then it goes back into the pan
for another 10 minutes or so.

While the ketchup is cooking and reducing, prepare the
bottles (see Tip). Fill your hot bottles with the hot ketchup.
Seal the tops while hot and label once cold. I have kept this
for up to two years.

FRUIT JAM

MAKES 4–5 450G (1 LB) JARS

I grow many soft fruits. They are delicious fresh when in season and also when preserved to enjoy all the year round in fruit jam. Once you have made your own jam, shop-bought versions will just not compare. My home-made fruit jam is equal fruit to sugar, and when you check the reverse label on some shop-bought jars the fruit content may be as little as 27%. Manufacturers may well add extra sugars as well as other ingredients to compensate for the natural acidity of the fruit.

This recipe is perfect and simple. I grow apricots but living in the north of England the climate is not perfect for them, so I may go several years before I get a good crop. When I do, I don't let a single one go to waste. I use this recipe for raspberries, blackberries and stoned fruits such as plums, damsons and greengages, too. Stoning can be difficult, especially if the fruits are small, so after weighing the fruits I count them into the pan and then count out of the pan the same number of stones.

1kg fresh fruits, stoned
1kg granulated sugar
   or jam sugar
Zest and juice of
   1 large lemon
Knob of butter
   (if needed)

You will need:
Large preserving pan
   or casserole dish
Digital weighing scales
Lemon zester
Clean tea towel
2 tea plates or saucers
Wooden spoon
Timer
4–5 x 450g (1lb) clean
   glass jars with lids
Jam funnel (optional)

Start the night before. Place the fruits into the large pan, sprinkling over the sugar, lemon zest and juice as you go along. Cover the pan with a cloth then transfer to a cool place (not the fridge) and leave overnight.

The next day uncover the pan – some of the sugar will have already dissolved amongst the fruits and they will be sitting in a pool of syrup. Place the pan over a low heat on the hob. Place a couple of tea plates or saucers in the freezer. Stir the fruits from time to time and once the mixture has lost its grittiness, the sugar has dissolved and the fruits are swimming around in sugar syrup, turn up the heat. If you are making a jam from stoned plums, damsons or greengages, any stones that you have missed will float to the surface and can be removed using a spoon. Bring the mixture to a fast boil then pop on your timer and boil for 15 minutes, stirring occasionally.

Recipe continued overleaf

TIP
I have made this jam using less sugar. Make this with 850g sugar instead of 1kg. It will yield a more fruity jam, though it will not preserve as well. It will keep for 1 month on the shelf or freeze in jars and thaw overnight in the fridge when needed.

While the jam is bubbling away, sterilise your jars. Wash them in warm soapy water, rinse but do not dry them. Transfer to a rack upside down and place in a cold oven, then turn the oven on to 100°C, allowing the jars and the oven to come up to temperature. Keep the oven on for 10 minutes then turn it off but leave the jars inside until your jam is ready. Jar lids can be sterilised by covering them in cold water in a small saucepan, bring them to the boil and boil for 2–3 minutes. Pour off the water and allow to cool down. Alternatively, use the microwave (page 231).

After the jam has boiled for 15 minutes it will have reduced and be quite thick. Turn off the heat and take one of the plates from the freezer. Place about 1 tablespoon of the very hot jam onto the very cold plate and pop it into the fridge for a minute or two. Take from the fridge and push your index finger through the jam. If it wrinkles and is gloopy and your finger leaves a trail, then your jam is done and will set when cold. If, however, your jam is still runny and the trail from your finger immediately fills, boil it for a further 5 minutes and repeat.

Stir the jam thoroughly and if there is a scum on the surface (apricots especially!) then add the knob of butter and stir through until the scum disperses.

Divide between the hot sterilised jars, add the lids while hot then label when cold.

JAM TARTS

MAKES 12

I love a jam tart and I have included this recipe for several reasons. It took me years to fathom out how to get them right and I was thrilled when I did – so I just had to share them with you.

200–250g shortcrust pastry dough (I save offcuts in the freezer until I have 200g)

350g favourite jam, plus 3–4 tbsp water

You will need:

2 sheets food grade plastic (I reuse cereal packet liners)

Rolling pin

8cm (3 inch) round cutter

2 identical 12-hole tart tins (one brushed with Lining Paste – see page 86) in the holes and the other brushed ever so lightly on the underside of the cups

Microwave-safe jug

Spoon

TIP

If you need to pause, or you feel the dough is becoming too warm, just slide the plastic-covered dough onto a baking sheet and chill in the fridge for 10 minutes.

Lay out a single sheet of cereal packet liner on the work surface, lay over the ball of pastry dough, flatten with the heel of your hand then cover with the second sheet. Take the rolling pin and begin to roll the dough – starting from the middle and working outwards. Roll out the dough to a large circle the thickness of a £1 coin. At this stage pop into the fridge to firm up.

In the meantime preheat the oven to 200°C/180°C fan/ 390°F/gas 5.

Take the chilled dough from the fridge and once on the work surface peel off the top sheet of plastic. Use the cutter to cut out 12 rounds, re-rolling the dough as necessary (see Tip). Peel the rounds from the bottom plastic then line the 12 holes of the greased tart tin.

When ready to bake take the second identical tart tin where the base of the cups have already been greased to prevent them sticking to the shells. Lay the second tray over the chilled shells very gently and without pushing down. Slide into the preheated oven and bake for 12 minutes. When the baking time is up, remove the two trays to a heatproof surface and carefully lift off the top tray. The pastry shells need to be golden brown and baked through. If the shells lack colour, pop them back into the oven uncovered for 3–4 minutes to complete their bake. Leave the baked shells in the tin while you prepare the jam filling.

Put the jam in a microwave-safe jug with the water. Microwave in 30-second bursts, stirring between each burst until the jam gets hot and to a pouring consistency.

Carefully fill each warm pastry shell to the brim with jam then leave to cool. There you have it – top-end tarts!

CONVERSION CHART

WEIGHT

IMPERIAL	METRIC
½oz	15g
1oz	29g
2oz	57g
3oz	85g
4oz	113g
5oz	141g
6oz	170g
8oz	227g
10oz	283g
12oz	340g
13oz	369g
14oz	397g
15oz	425g
1lb	453g

TEMPERATURE

FAHRENHEIT	CELSIUS
100 °F	37 °C
150 °F	65 °C
200 °F	93 °C
250 °F	121 °C
300 °F	150 °C
325 °F	160 °C
350 °F	180 °C
375 °F	190 °C
400 °F	200 °C
425 °F	220 °C
450 °F	230 °C
500 °F	260 °C
525 °F	274 °C
550 °F	288 °C

VOLUME

CUP	FLUID OUNCES	MILLILITRES	TABLESPOONS
8 cups	65 fl oz	1900ml	128
6 cups	48 fl oz	1420ml	96
5 cups	40 fl oz	1180ml	80
4 cups	32 fl oz	960ml	64
2 cups	16 fl oz	480ml	32
1 cup	8 fl oz	240ml	16
¾ cup	6 fl oz	180ml	12
⅔ cup	5 fl oz	160ml	11
½ cup	4 fl oz	120ml	8
⅜ cup	3 fl oz	90ml	6
⅓ cup	2.5 fl oz	80ml	5.5
¼ cup	2 fl oz	60ml	4
⅛ cup	1 fl oz	30ml	2
1/16 cup	½ fl oz	15ml	1

INDEX

jam tarts 243
mini Simnel cakes 168
jelly, simple sherry trifle
196, 198–9
juniper berries
beef in beer 64
cranberry roast 186–7

K

kale
all-veggie curry 32
serve up a savoury
soufflé 161–2
ketchup, fruit 238–9
kitchen tips 10–11
kneading 72
'knocking back' 73

L

lamb 128
universal cottage pie 27–8
lasagne **124**, 125
leek
coq au leekie bean
stew 138
instant veggie stock
cubes 206
leek & potato soup 60
leftovers 13, 14–49, 152
lemon 10
baked lemon cheesecake 113
courgette cupcakes 108
lemon delicious pudding
154, **155**
lemon and elderflower
cordial 177
lemon sponge pudding 150
lemon/lime icing 108, **109**
mini Simnel cakes 167–8

savoury stuffing
crowd-pleaser 192
lentil(s), universal cottage
pie 27–8
lime
baked lime, chocolate
& coconut cheesecake
110, 111–13
courgette cupcakes 108
lemon/lime icing 108, **109**
lining paste 152
liquid, reducing by half 141

M

maple syrup
granola 225
overnight oats 222
spiced bread 104
marinades 179–80
marshmallows **48**, 49
marzipan, mini Simnel cakes 168
meat
potted meats 16, **17**
see also beef; lamb; pork;
sausage meat
mint
baked stuffed tomatoes 41
mint salad 237
mint sauce 20, 237
minted pea puree 20
two-ingredient chocolate
pots 144
mixed spice
Eccles cakes 165–6
fruit loaf 99
gluten-free bread & butter
pudding 35–6
Jamaican-style ginger
cake 102

mini Simnel cakes 167–8
quick banana muffins 100
spiced bread 104
mocha log 203
muesli 221
overnight oats 222, **223**
muffins (cakes), quick
banana 100, **101**
muffins (English) 88, **89**
multi-cookers, cleaning tips 11
mushroom
30-minute chicken
& mushrooms 66, **67**
'all-in-one' beef
bourguignon 62
baked stuffed tomatoes 41
cider chicken with
mushrooms & tarragon
130, **131**
cranberry roast 186–7
mushroom soup 53
universal cottage pie 27–8

N

nutmeg
12-hour slow-cooked
ragu 121–2
30-minute chicken
& mushrooms 66
'all-in-red' braised
red cabbage 185
baked stuffed tomato 41
courgette cannelloni 29–30
Eccles cakes 165–6
gluten-free bread &
butter pudding 35–6
lasagne 125
leek & potato soup 60
muesli 221

slow-roast crispy belly
pork **178**, 179–80
potato
all-veggie curry 32
curried ham croquettes 24, **25**
fishcakes **18**, 19–20
instant veggie stock
cubes 206
leek & potato soup 60
potato & onion soup 60
roasted potato, garlic &
rosemary soup 58, **59**
universal cottage pie **26**, 27–8
potted meats 16, **17**
preserving methods **230**, 231–6
see also freezing food
proving 72–4
prune(s)
peppered pork with fruit:
casserole version 182
peppered pork with fruit:
oven version 184
puff pastry
Eccles cakes **164**, 165–6
hands-free puff pastry 211
two-salmon plait **158**, 159–60
puree, minted pea 20

R
radish, mint salad 237
ragu
12-hour slow-cooked
ragu **120**, 121–2
lasagne 125
raisin(s)
flexi sticky toffee
pudding 151–2
fruit ketchup 238–9
granola 225

mini Simnel cakes 167–8
raspberry
gluten-free bread &
butter pudding 35–6
granola Sunday sundae 226
overnight oats 222
raspberry & almond bread
& butter pudding 34
simple sherry trifle 198–9
two-ingredient chocolate
pots 144
ready meals 8–9, 52
red cabbage coleslaw 194, **195**
red wine
12-hour slow-cooked
ragu 121–2
'all-in-one' beef
bourguignon 62
courgette cannelloni 29–30
rhubarb, offcuts pudding 38
roulade, strawberries
& cream 173
rum, spiced bread 104
runner bean, pickled
beans 236

S
sage leaves, savoury stuffing
crowd-pleaser 192
salads
beetroot 170, **171**
fresh tomato 172
greenhouse 40
mint 237
salmon
fishcakes **18**, 19–20
two-salmon plait **158**, 159–60
salt 10
sardine(s), fishcakes **18**, 19–20

sauces
all-in-one cranberry 187
apple 181
caramel 151–2, **153**
for chicken stir-fry 126–7
espresso 212
for lasagne **124**, 125
mint 237
white 30
sausage meat, savoury stuffing
crowd-pleaser 192, **193**
seasonal recipes 157–203
'seasoning to taste' 10
seed(s)
granola 225
muesli 221
overnight oats 222
shallot
'all-in-one' beef
bourguignon 62
cider chicken with
mushrooms & tarragon 130
sherry trifle **196**, 198–9
shortcrust pastry, jam tarts 243
'Showstopper' angel food
cake **174**, 175–6
soft cheese, two-salmon
plait 159–60
souffle, serve up a savoury
161–2, **163**
soups 51–60
carrot & coriander 54, **55**
leek & potato 60
mushroom 53
parsnip 56–7
parsnip & apple 57
potato & onion 60
spaghetti Bolognese 122, **123**
spiced bread 104

ACKNOWLEDGEMENTS

My first full colour book! Wow...

When the proposal for this book had been accepted, the real work then started. I began with an outline, then a set of notes and ultimately a daily commitment which usually started around 5.30 a.m. for around four hours and continued for many months.

An early start works for me – the words flow and the time just flies by. I have found that in order to avoid 'writer's block' I have to leave my work at a stage where I know where I am going next. I enjoy writing, but it can feel solitary and at times a lonely place. Even though I now hold this gorgeous book in my hand – my mind is taken back to those dark early winter mornings and I recall struggling to organise my head when a full-colour cookbook seemed a giant piece of work. I remember thinking – 'I have so much to write about!'

Who would ever have thought I could give myself the title 'author' and at the age of 70 – unbelievable. Transferring my head full of words onto paper and into this amazing book makes me feel very proud. However, as any author will agree, it may be one name on the cover but a book is the result of a team commitment, a strict timetable adhered to by many and a shared vision for the finished piece of work.

Seeing my work transfer to the pages of this book and made available to readers worldwide is remarkable but, as the saying goes, 'There is no I in TEAM' and so many individuals have ensured this book is here.

I would like to thank you all:

To 'him indoors' (Tim) for the early morning hot drinks and for always reminding me of what is important in life. I could do none of this without you and maybe I don't tell you often enough.

To Geraldine, Anna and Kate (Yellow Poppy Media) who have been by my side for many years. You know me so well, understand what is right for me and I respect your professional approach. Those many phone conversations, coffee chats, lunches and many meetings in and out of hours. Thank you for always being there.

To Hockley, Katy, Sian, Amy and Lizzy at Bluebird for trusting me to write another book. Straightforward timetabling, not forgetting those regular Zoom sessions where we thrashed out the detail. Oh, and this time I was able to enjoy the fab make-up, hair and food photography sessions with a great team. There will also be people involved that I haven't had the pleasure to meet – you know who you are and thank you.

Last but not least, thank you to all of the readers of this book – the recipes in here are some of my favourites – I hope they become yours too!

– Nancy

First published 2025 by One Boat
an imprint of Pan Macmillan
The Smithson, 6 Briset Street, London EC1M 5NR
EU representative: Macmillan Publishers Ireland Ltd, 1st Floor,
The Liffey Trust Centre, 117–126 Sheriff Street Upper,
Dublin 1, D01 YC43

Associated companies throughout the world
www.panmacmillan.com

ISBN 978-1-0350-4448-1

1 3 5 7 9 8 6 4 2
A CIP catalogue record for this book is available from the British Library.
Printed and bound in China

Art Direction & Text Design: Smith & Gilmour
Cover Design: Siobhan Hooper, Pan Macmillan Art Department
Photography: Clare Winfield
Food Styling: Kathy Kordalis
Prop Styling: Jenny Iggleden
Hair & Make-up: Clare Wood

Visit www.panmacmillan.com to read more about all our books
and to buy them. You will also find features, author interviews and
news of any author events, and you can sign up for e-newsletters
so that you're always first to hear about our new releases.